Table of Contents

Projects

Wired Micro-Macramé Jewelry
A Gallery of Designs and Inspiration

For many years, I've had a love affair with beads and fibers and my favorite mode of creative expression has been through micro-macramé jewelry. But in addition to the familiar materials like cords and beads, I've frequently relied on wire to enhance my jewelry designs. Wire has always been a valuable material to me for translating my ideas into form. I've found that even the simplest wire elements when used as armatures, ornaments, and clasps can add shape and style to a micro-macramé design. The combination of these two versatile techniques will add a distinctive look to jewelry while expanding the design potential.

The examples in this gallery show some of the ways I've used wire elements in my jewelry designs. In my necklace called "Shell Music", I used soldered wire to frame the free-form knotting. The rest of the examples here feature simple wire forms shaped with pliers and textured with a hammer.

The jewelry projects included in this book will take you beyond basic micro-macramé and will introduce you to ways in which you can use simple wirework to shape, support and enhance your micro-macramé jewelry designs. The wirework used in the projects is not complex, however this book is not intended as an overall introduction to wirework. Previous knowledge of basic wirework is recommended. By the same token, the projects are intermediate level and a working knowledge of macramé techniques is required. My first book, "Micro-Macramé Jewelry, Tips & Techniques for Knotting with Beads" and my DVD are both great resources for the beginning knotter.

It's my hope that this book will teach you some new techniques, and inspire you to express your creativity with fibers, wires, and beads!

"Shell Music" - Intuitive free-form knotting within a copper wire frame

Macramé earrings with hammered wire paddles

Wired
Micro-Macramé Jewelry

Enhancing Fiber Designs with Wire

by

Joan R. Babcock

Graphic Design by Jeff Babcock

ISBN 978-0-9773052-2-3

Published by:

Joan Babcock Designs
16 Camerada Rd.
Santa Fe, NM, 87508-8766

www.joanbabcock.com

www.micro-macramejewelry.com

First Printing - March 2010

A man is a bundle of relations,
a knot of roots,
whose flower and fruitage is the world

- Ralph Waldo Emerson

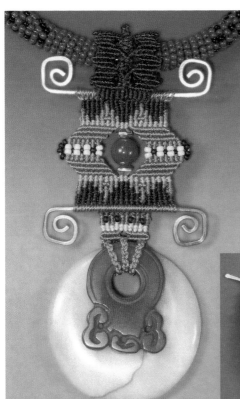

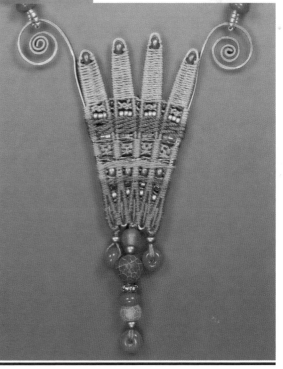

"Painted Desert" A twisted wire armature gives support and shape to this necklace

"Geometric Pendant" - This peice features wire bars for structure and as design elements

"Butterfly Brooch" Gracefully curved wires suggest a butterfly's wings and antennae

"Tree of Life" A rounded wire armature suggests the canopy of a tree

" Bands of Gold" Shaped wire is used as a frame for knotted and twined fiber and thin gauge wire

Materials

1. Knotting Board - I recommend an 11" X 17" "macramé project board" (by Pepperell Crafts) made of **particle board** and wrapped in plastic. Leave the plastic intact to avoid the fibers shedding onto your clothing. Another option is a rigid **cork board**, ⅜" thick or thicker, sold as a "frameless bulletin board" at many craft stores.

2. Pins - Use sturdy quilting or sewing pins that have a thin shank but do not bend too easily. The smaller size T-pins (1.25") are also fine, but avoid using the larger size T-pins (1.75"), they are too thick for micro-macramé and may damage the cord.

3. Size #2 Crewel Embroidery Needle - They are about 2" long and have an opening that is large enough for the cord. Having needles in a few in different sizes for different uses is helpful.

4. Scissors - I recommend that you invest in a high quality pair that is sharp and small enough to get into tight places.

5. Clear Nail Polish - I use this to coat finishing knots and prevent them from coming undone. It can also be used to stiffen the ends of cord and prevent the cord from unraveling.

6. Fray Check - For ease in threading beads onto the nylon cord, coat about an inch at the end with Fray Check and let dry for 10 - 15 minutes. Snip off the tip at a sharp angle. This creates a "needle" and makes it easier to pass the cord through the bead. Fray Check is found at fabric stores.

7. Wireworking Pliers - For these projects I recommend: standard chain nose (narrow tip preferred), standard round nose, flat nose, and flush cutters.

8. Chasing Hammer and Hammering Block - I like the look of hammered wire, however most of the projects do not require that you planish (flatten) the wire if that's your preference.

9. Ruler - Flat metal preferred.

10. Bead Reamer - Macrame cord is thick and some bead holes will need to be enlarged.

11. Renaissance Wax (optional) - I apply a coating of this wax on wire (brass and copper especially) to prevent oxidation and dulling of the metal over time.

12. 18 gauge Nylon Cord - I used SuperLon Bead/Macrame cord and C-Lon #18 cord interchangeably in these projects. See each project's title page for a specific list of cord lengths.

13. Round Wire 14, 16, 18, 20, and 22 gauge (28 - 30g colored copper is also used in the Sunrise Pin)- Copper, Brass, or Sterling Silver that is half-hard or dead-soft. See each project's title page for a specific list of required wire.

14. Beads - See each project's title page for a suggested list of beads. You can substitute beads of your own choosing for the beads that I've used in any project, as long as they are the same general size and have large enough holes for the cord.

Knots and Terms

The following are the terms and abbreviations that are used in this book:

KC - Knotting Cord : The active cord that wraps around another (anchor) cord.

AC - Anchor Cord : The passive cord which holds the Knotting Cord.

Warp Cords - all working cords (except the **AC**)

MTK - Mounting Knot (see diagram)

DHH - Double Half Hitch Use this diagram for Double Half Hitches that are made horizontally or diagonally. The angle of the **AC** determines the angle of the row of knots.

VDHH - Vertical Double Half Hitch This is the same knot as a horizontal **DHH**, however the **AC** is vertical rather than horizontal.

AHHch - Alternating Half Hitch Chain - A series of **HHs** done on 2 cords, alternating back and forth from cord to cord.

LHKch - Lark's Head Knot Chain - A series of **HHs** made with the **KC** going over, under, over, under, and so on around an **AC**.

OVK - Overhand Knot (see diagram)

SQK - Square Knot The diagram shows a **SQK** with two anchor or "filler" cords, however they can be made with only one or with several anchor cords. A **"Flat" Square Knot** is a **SQK** made with 2 knotting cords but omitting the 2 anchor cords. It is used to tie off cords at the back of a piece.

Square Knot (SQK)

Mounting Hitch (MH) 1 - 2   Mounting Knot (MTK) 1 - 4

Double Half Hitch (DHH)

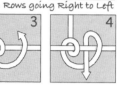

← Rows going Right to Left

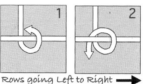

Rows going Left to Right →

Vertical Double Half Hitch (VDHH)

← Rows going Right to Left

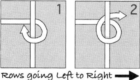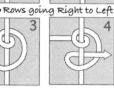

Rows going Left to Right →

Alternating Half Hitch Chain (AHHch)

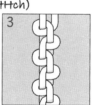

Lark's Head Knot Chain (LHKch)

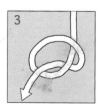

Overhand Knot (OVK)

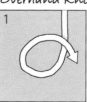

Anacara Earrings

These earrings are one of my favorites styles and one of the quickest projects to complete. The curvy and angular spiral dangles add dimension and movement.

Materials

Wire:
- (4") 18g. round wire
- (8.5") 20g. round wire

18g. Nylon cord:
- Color 1 - 2 lengths @ 20"
- Color 2 - 2 lengths @ 20"
- Color 3 - 2 lengths @ 20"
- Color 4 - 2 lengths @ 20"
- Color 5 - 2 lengths @ 20" (This color is used as the AC & will only show a bit at the edges)

Beads:
The following beads were used in the project, others may be substituted if desired.
- (20) 11° seed beads
- (2) 4 mm drops
- (2) 10 mm crystal teardrops
- (2) 6 mm round
- (2) 5 mm metal spacers
- (2) 8° seed beads

Other:
- (2) earring wires

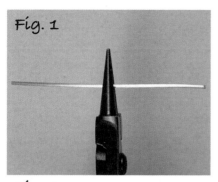

Fig. 1

Fig. 2

A. B. C. D.
INCHES 1

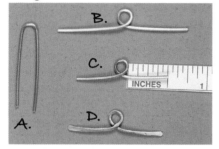

Fig. 3

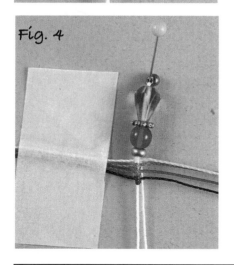

Fig. 4

Part 1 - Shaping the Wire Bars

1. Cut a 2" piece of 18g. wire. Grasp it at the middle with round nose pliers. It should be positioned approx. $\frac{1}{4}$" from the tips of the pliers (see Fig. 1).

2. Hold firmly and move both ends of the wire toward the other to form a "U" shape (see Fig. 2a). Cross the wire ends over each other and move them in opposite directions so that they come straight out to the sides (see Fig. 2b).

3. Trim each "leg" with flush cutters to approx. $\frac{1}{2}$" (see Fig. 2c). Flatten with a hammer. Splay the ends by bringing the hammer down and outward with each stroke as if you were flattening the wire and brushing it at the same time (see Fig. 2d).

4. Smooth the ends with a file, sand paper, or rotary tool. Form the other wire bar just like the first.

Part 2 - Knotting Directions

1. Divide your cords in half and use one cord of each color for the first earring. Select Color #5 and thread a drop bead onto it, positioning it at the center of the cord. Bring the two cord ends together.

2. Thread the "drop" beads onto the two joined cords starting with the bottom bead and working up (see Fig. 3). Pin to the board with the cords hanging downward. These two cords will be used as the Anchor Cords (**AC**) - one for the right half of the earring and the other for the left.

3. Take the remaining four cords and tape them to the board (at the approximate center of the cords), just to the left of the 2 vertical **AC**s (see Fig. 4).

4. Starting at the top next to the bead, attach each of the cords to the left hand **AC** using Vertical Double Half Hitches (**VDHH**) (see Fig. 4). **Note** - the top cord color will be at the outside edge of the earring, the bottom will be at the inside edge.

5. Attach the four cords to the right hand **AC** with **VDHH**s (see Fig. 5). Rotate the **AC**s to the left horizontally and pin to the board (see Fig. 6). Thread (2) 11° seed beads onto the outermost cord (nearest the drop beads).

Project One

6. Bring the lower **AC** around to the right at a slight diagonal angle and make a row of Double Half Hitches (**DHH**). Use the beads to determine the correct angle of the row - the last **DHH** should rest snug against the beads (see Fig. 6).

7. Make an Overhand Knot (**OVK**) in the **AC** at the edge of the row next to the **DHH** (see Fig. 6). Bring the **AC** back around to the left and make a row of **DHH**s parallel to and identical to the previous row (see Fig. 7). **Tip** - Rotate the piece as often as necessary to attain the easiest position for knotting.

8. Thread one 11° seed bead onto the outermost cord. Bring the **AC** around to the right at a slight diagonal angle and make a row of **DHHs**. Use the bead to determine the correct angle of the row (see Fig. 8).

9. Position the piece so the drop beads are vertical and facing up. Make an **OVK** in the **AC** at the edge of the row next to the last knot. Bring the **AC** back around to the left and make a row of **DHHs** parallel to the previous row (see Fig. 9).

10. Thread (2) 11° seed beads onto the outermost cord. Bring the **AC** around to the right at a slight diagonal angle and make a row of **DHH**. This row of **DHHs** should be at a right angle to the drop beads (see Fig. 10).

11. Make an **OVK** in the **AC** at the edge of the row next to the last knot. Bring the **AC** back around to the left and make a row of **DHHs** parallel to the previous row (see Fig. 11).

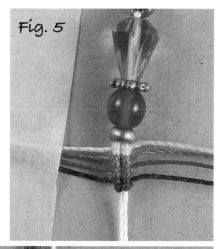

Fig. 5

Fig. 6

Fig. 7

Fig. 8

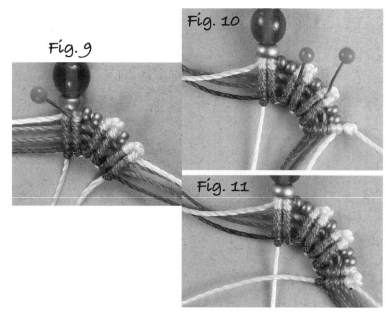

Fig. 9

Fig. 10

Fig. 11

Wired Micro-Macramé Jewelry

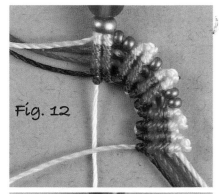

Fig. 12

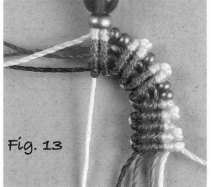

Fig. 13

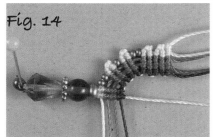

Fig. 14

Fig. 15

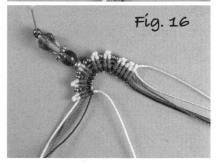

Fig. 16

12. Bring the **AC** back to the right and make a horizontal row of **DHH**s. Make an **OVK** in the **AC** at the edge of the row next to the last knot. Bring the **AC** back around to the left and make a row of **DHH**s parallel to and identical to the previous row (see Fig. 12).

13. Bring the **AC** back to the right and make a horizontal row of **DHH**s. Make a very tight **OVK** at the end of the row (see Fig. 13). **Tip** - to tighten an **OVK**, grip the cord next to the knot with chain nose pliers. Push upwards towards the knot with the pliers while pulling out on the cord.

14. Knot the other half of the earring in a mirror image of the completed half (see Figures 14 - 18).

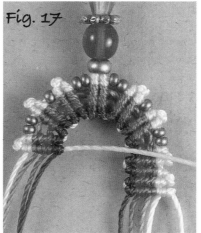

Fig. 17

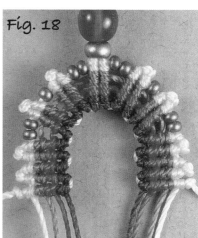

Fig. 18

Part 3-Attaching the Wire Bar and Finishing

1. Pin the earring to the board with the bottom pointing up. Bring the wire bar into position next to the bottom rows of knots. Starting with the middle right hand cord and working towards the edge, attach the bar to the earring with **DHH**s. Make sure that there isn't a gap between the knotted row and the bar. Repeat on the left side (see Figures 19 & 20).

2. Fold all of the cords to the back of the piece like a hem. Use a #10 sharps beading needle (or fine sewing needle) and a compatible colored thread to sew down the cords to the back of the earring (see Figures 21 & 22).

Note - Make your stitches in the "ditch" between the bar and the last row of knots. Be sure to catch every cord and secure them well!

Project One

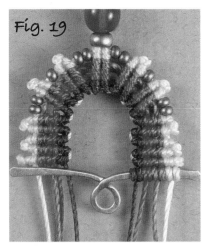

Fig. 19

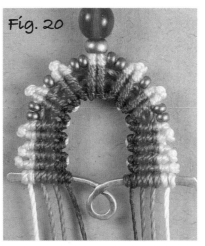

Fig. 20

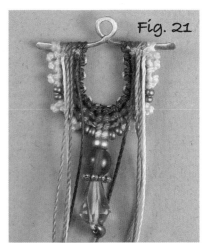

Fig. 21

3. Cut off the excess cords close to the stitching (see Fig. 22). Apply a small amount of clear nail polish over the stitching and let dry.

Wire Charm Centerpiece

1. For a round or a squared spiral charm, cut a 4.25" length of 20g. wire. Curl it to make a loose spiral at one end, until there is about ½" of straight wire remaining at the other end (see Fig. 23a and 23b). Make a backwards facing loop (see Fig. 23c and 23d).

2. Attach an earring wire around both the loop of the wire bar and the loop of the charm. Repeat all steps for the other earring.

Figure 24 shows the earring with a "Rounded Spiral" charm. Figure 25 shows the earring with a "Squared Spiral" charm.

Fig. 22

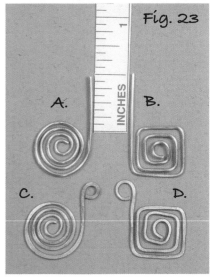

Fig. 23

A.   B.

C.   D.

Fig. 25

Fig. 24

Fandango Earrings

These earrings are unique and fun to wear. They are also one of the easier projects to complete. In this project I'll show you how to make an "encased warps hem", a technique I developed to address the eternal macramé dilemma of - "what do I do with the leftover cords?"

Materials

Cord and Thread:
- 18g. Nylon Cord - 8 lengths @ 24" (2 ea. of 4 colors). In my sample I used 4 closely related colors with values that range from light to dark, thus creating an interesting optical effect.

Wire:
- 2 lengths @ 3.75" of 18g. round wire (silver, brass, copper, or gold-filled)

Beads: (the following were used in the project, others may be substituted)
- (2) 6 mm round fire polish or crystal beads
- (16) 11° matte gold seed beads
- (30+) 11° seed beads
- (20 - 30) 11° or 13° Delicas
- (10) 4 mm round matte gold "Druk" beads

Other
- (2) Earring Wires

Project Two

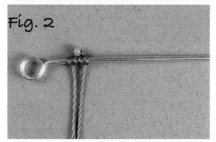

Fig. 1 A. B.

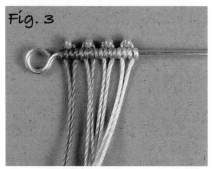

Fig. 2

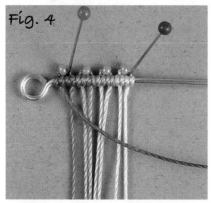

Fig. 3

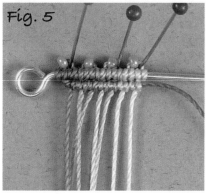

Fig. 4

Fig. 5

Part 1 - The Wire

1. Cut a 3 ¾" length of wire. Make a 90° bend ½" from one end (see Fig. 1a).

2. Take the tip of the ½" bent wire and grasp it with the round nose pliers (about halfway down from the tips). Bend the wire back toward center making a loop (see Fig. 1b). Make an identical loop in the other wire.

3. Optional - Apply a thin coat of Renaissance wax to the wires with a soft cloth. This helps to prevent tarnishing and is especially useful for brass and copper.

Part 2 - Knotting the Half-Circle Design

Directions for the left-facing earring:

1. Attach four of the nylon cords to the wire as follows: Thread an 11° seed bead onto the cord and position the bead at the middle of the cord. Fold the cord in half so that the ends meet. Make a **MTK** (Mounting Knot) around the wire, keeping the bead top/center at all times (see Fig. 2). Note that the wire loop should be on the left.

2. Attach the all of the cords in the same way. Tighten the **MTK**s well and push all of the cords neatly together. The first **MTK** should be positioned just to the side of the loop (see Fig. 3).

3. Pin the piece horizontally to the board, beads at the top and cords hanging down (see Fig.4).

4. Bring the first cord on the left (serving as the Anchor Cord or **AC**) horizontally to the right just below the wire (see Fig. 4). Make a row of 7 Double Half Hitches (**DHH**s) around it keeping the row parallel to the wire (see Fig. 5). The same **AC** will be used throughout the piece. I will refer to the 7 remaining cords (a.k.a.warp cords) as Cds. #1 - 7, going from left to right.

5. Bring the **AC** back towards the left at a slight (about 35°) angle. Working from right to left , make **DHH**s around the **AC** with Cds. #7 & 6 (see Fig. 6).

6. Thread (1) 11° bead onto Cd #5. Attach the cord to the **AC** with a **DHH** (see Fig. 7).

7. Attach Cd #4 to the **AC** with a **DHH**.

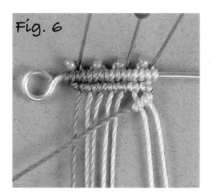

Fig. 6

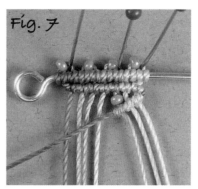

Fig. 7

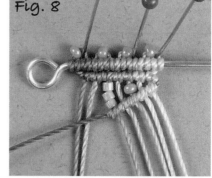

Fig. 8

8. Thread (3) 13° Delica seed beads onto Cd #3. Attach the cord to the **AC** with a **DHH** (see Fig. 8).

9. Attach Cd #2 to the **AC** with a **DHH** (see Fig. 9).

10. Thread (1) 11°, (1) 4mm rd. bead, & (1) 11° onto Cd #1. Attach the cord to the **AC** with a **DHH** (see Fig. 9).

Note - You have completed one V-shaped section. There will be a total of five V-shaped sections that will form the half-circle.

11. Thread (1) 11° bead onto the **AC** (see Fig. 9). Push the 11° bead up to the edge of the last **DHH**. Bring the **AC** back to the right and make a row of **DHH**s just below and parallel to the one above (see Fig. 10).

Note - If you are having trouble getting the first **DHH** of this row to sit tight against the previous row, try moving the 11° bead slightly away from the edge before making the first **DHH** of the row. That will make it easier to get the knot tighter to the previous row. Now pull the **AC** and the 11° bead snug against the outer edge.

12. Repeat Steps #5 - 11 three times. Repeat Steps #5 - 10 one time. You should have a total of five V-shaped sections (see Fig. 11). Unpin and reposition the piece as you go along to maintain the most comfortable angle for knotting.

13. Pin the piece to the board with the knotted half circle at the top. The wire bar should be horizontal and the loop should be to the right. Thread a 6 mm bead onto the wire and position it at the center. Position all 7 warp cords and the **AC** behind the wire bar (see Fig. 12).

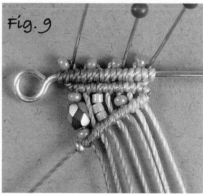

Fig. 9

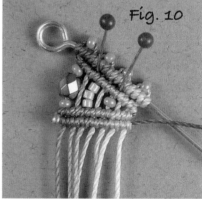

Fig. 10

Fig. 11

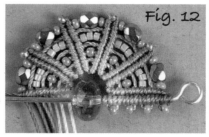

Fig. 12

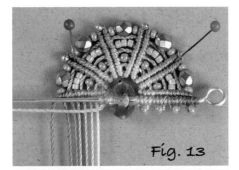

Fig. 13

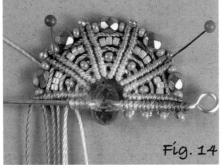

Fig. 14

Fig. 15

Fig. 16

Fig. 17

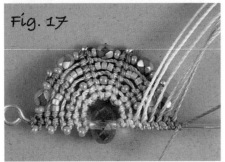

14. The **AC** (on the left) will be considered Cd #1 and the 7 warp cords will be Cds #2 - 8. Knot Cd #8 onto the wire bar with a **DHH**. Now bring the tail of Cd #8 horizontally to the left, parallel to the wire bar (see Fig. 13).

15. Treating Cd #8 and the wire bar as one single unit, make a **DHH** around them with Cd #7. Bring the tail of Cd #8 to the back of the piece **behind** all the remaining warp cords and out of the way (see Fig. 14).

16. Now bring Cd #7 horizontally to the left, parallel to the wire bar. Treat Cd #7 and the wire bar as a single unit. Make a **DHH** around them with the Cd #6. Bring the tail of Cd #7 to the back of the piece **behind** the remaining warp cords and out of the way (see Fig. 15).

17. Bring Cd #6 horizontally to the left, parallel to the wire bar. Treat this cord and the wire bar as a single unit. Make a **DHH** around them with Cd #5. Bring Cd #6 to the back of the piece and out of the way (see Fig. 16 for Steps 17 - 21).

18. Bring Cd #5 horizontally to the left, parallel to the wire bar. Treat this cord and the wire bar as a single unit. Make a **DHH** around them with Cd #4. Bring Cd #5 to the back of the piece and out of the way.

19. Bring Cd #4 horizontally to the left, parallel to the wire bar. Treat this cord and the wire bar as a single unit. Make a **DHH** around them with Cd #3. Bring Cd #4 to the back of the piece and out of the way.

20. Bring Cd #3 horizontally to the left, parallel to the wire bar. Treat this cord and the wire bar as a single unit. Make a **DHH** around them with Cd #2. Bring Cd #3 to the back of the piece and out of the way.

21. Bring Cd #2 horizontally to the left, parallel to the wire bar. Treat this cord and the wire bar as a single unit. Make a **DHH** around them with Cd #1. Bring Cd #2 to the back of the piece and out of the way.

22. Flip the piece so that the back is facing you (see Fig. 17). Carefully cut off Cds #3 - 8 very close to the knotting (see Fig. 18). Do not cut off Cds #1 & 2! (These are the 2 cords closest to the outside edge.) Pay special attention to cutting off Cd #3 very close and neat so that it doesn't leave a visible nub that may be seen from the front of the earring.

23. Use a #10 sharps beading needle (or fine sewing needle) and matching thread to tack down Cds. #1 & 2 to the back of the earring. Sew through and over both cords several times to secure them (see Fig. 19). Apply a dab of clear nail polish, let dry, and cut off the excess cord.

Fig. 18

Part 3 - Finishing

1. Grip the wire with the tips of your chainnose pliers at the bottom edge of the knotting. Make a 45° bend in the wire facing backwards in the direction of the knotted half circle (see Fig. 20).

2. Make a tight spiral in the wire, bending it in the direction of the front of the earring (see Fig. 21).

Fig. 19

Fig. 20

Fig. 21

Completing the right-facing earring:

3. The right-facing earring is a mirror image of the left-facing earring. I suggest that you pin the left-facing earring to the board so that you can frequently refer to it while making the second earring (see Figures 22 & 23).

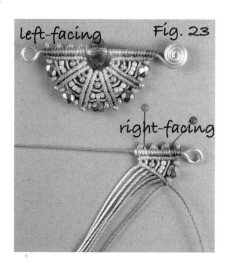

left-facing   Fig. 23

right-facing

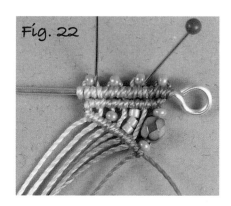

Fig. 22

Winter Solstice Earrings

These unique and fanciful earrings look great by themselves or when paired with the Dynasty Pendant.

Materials

Wire:
- (9") 18 gauge round wire
- (5") 20 gauge round wire

Cord:
18g. Nylon Cord:
- 2 lengths @ 40" Outer ring
- 2 lengths @ 28" Middle ring
- 2 lengths @ 24" Inner ring

Beads: the following were used in the project, others may be substituted.
- (2) 11-12 mm crystal teardrops
- (44) 8° seed beads
- (44) 1.5 mm cube beads
- (16) 11° seed beads

Other:
- (2) Earring wires
- Embroidery needle (narrow)
- Sharps #10 beading needle
- Beading thread in compatible color to the cord

Fig. 1

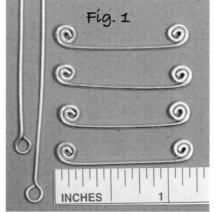

Fig. 2

Fig. 3

Fig. 3A

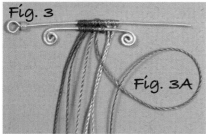

Fig. 4

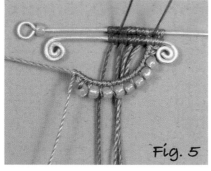

Fig. 5

Part 1 - Forming the Wire Shapes

1. Cut (4) 2.25" lengths of 18g. wire, and shape them all in the following way: At each end of the wire, make tight closed spirals, gradually curling them in until the length is 1.25" long (see Fig. 1).

2. Cut (2) 2.5" lengths of 20g. wire. Make an eyepin loop on one end of each (see Fig. 1).

Each earring will use 2 of the 18g. and 1 of the 20g. wires.

Part 2 - The Knotted and Beaded Center

1. Thread (1) 8° bead onto the 20g. wire (see Fig. 2).

2. Double (1) 24", (1) 28", and (1) 40" cord, and attach each to the 20g. wire with **MTK** (Mounting Knots). The 24" cord will be on the left , the 28" in the middle, the 40" on the right (see Fig. 2).

3. Attach an 18g. wire segment directly below the 20g. wire using **DHH**s (Double Half Hitches) in the following way: **A.** Pin the piece to the board or hold it in your hand, whatever you find to be easier. **B.** Place the new wire on top of the warp cords. Start with the left hand cord and work towards the right. **C.** To form a **HH**, make a loop to the right side of the wire with the knotting cord (see Fig. 3A). **D.** Slip the loop over the end of the wire and into place, then tighten it up. Repeat with another **HH** to form a complete **DHH**.

4. Slide the wires into position (see Fig. 4). Pin the piece to the board between the rows (see Fig. 5).

5. Using the outer right hand cord as the **KC** (Knotting Cord) and the adjacent cord as the **AC** (Anchor Cord), make a **LHK** (Lark's Head Knot) **Chain** in the following way: **A.** Thread (8) 8° seed beads onto the **KC**. Make an Overhand knot at the very end of the cord so they won't slide off. **B.** Make (1) **HH** under the **AC**, (1) **HH** over it, (1) under, and (1) over. (Note - the order of the "under & over" is reversed from a typical **LHK** chain to achieve a different look). **C.** Slide a bead up the cord. **D.** Make (1) **HH** under the **AC**, and (1) **HH** over it. **E.** Slide a bead up the cord. **F.** Continue in the same way, finishing the chain with (1) **HH** under, (1) over, (1) under, and (1) over. (see Fig. 5).

Project Three

6. Position the piece with the chain and cords to the top and pin in place. Bring the outer right hand cord behind the 18g. segment and make a **DHH** around the wire. Bring the same cord behind the 20g. segment and make a **DHH** around the wire (see Fig. 6).

7. Thread (4) 11° seed beads onto the next right hand (upward facing) cord. Bring this cord behind the 18g. segment and make a **DHH** around the wire. Bring the same cord behind the 20g. segment and make a **DHH** around the wire (see Fig. 7).

8. Shape the next upward facing cord around the seed beads. Hold it in place with a pin if necessary. Bring it behind the 18g. segment and make a **DHH** around the wire. Bring the same cord behind the 20g. segment and make a **DHH** around the wire (see Fig. 8).

9. Thread (8) 1.5 mm cube beads onto the next upward facing cord. Bring it behind the 18g. segment and make a **DHH** around the wire. Bring the same cord behind the 20g. segment and make a **DHH** around the wire (see Fig. 9).

10. Attach the two **LHK** chain cords to the wires with **DHH**s (see Fig. 10). Slide the 20g. wire down into place.

11. Working from left to right, attach the remaining 18g. wire segment next to the 20g. segment with **DHH**s (see Fig. 11). Make sure that the wires are pulled tightly together without a gap between them.

12. Make a **LHK** chain with the 2 outer cords to match the first one (refer to Step #5) (see Fig. 12).

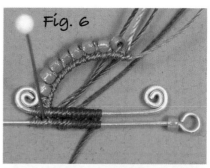

Fig. 6

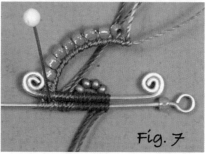

Fig. 7

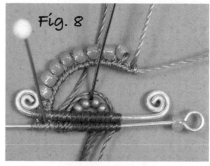

Fig. 8

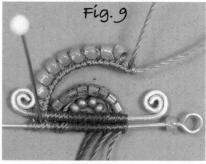

Fig. 9

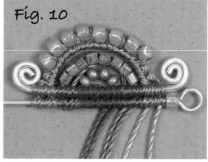

Fig. 10

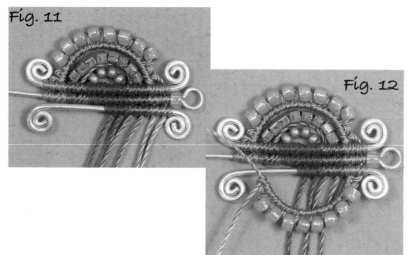

Fig. 11

Fig. 12

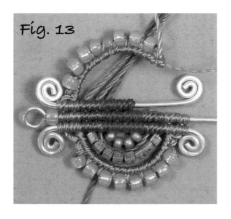

Fig. 13

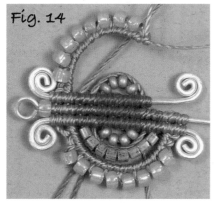

Fig. 14

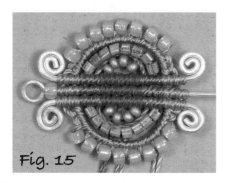

Fig. 15

Fig. 16

13. Reposition the piece with the new **LHK** chain to the top and pin in place. Bring the outer right (upward facing) cord behind the 18g. segment and make a **DHH** around the wire. Bring the tail of the cord between the wires and to the back of the piece (see Fig. 13).

14. Thread (4) 11° seed beads onto the next upward facing cord. Bring it behind the 18g. segment and make a **DHH** around the wire. Bring the cord to the back of the piece (see Fig. 14).

15. Shape the next upward facing cord around the seed beads. Hold it in place with a pin if necessary. Bring it behind the 18g. segment and make a **DHH** around the wire. Bring the cord to the back of the piece (see Fig. 14).

16. Thread (8) 1.5 mm cube beads onto the next upward facing cord. Bring it behind the 18g. segment and make a **DHH** around the wire. Bring the cord to the back of the piece (see Fig. 15).

17. Attach the two **LHK** chain cords to the wire with **DHH**s. Bring the cords to the back of the piece (see Fig. 15).

Part 3 - Finishing

1. Thread the outer cord onto a narrow embroidery needle. Sew it through the cord on the top of the adjacent **MTK** on the 20g. wire. Bring the cord to the back of the earring. Pull the 18g. and 20g. segments closely together. Make a tight Overhand knot in the cord to hold (see Fig. 16).

2. Thread beading thread onto a Sharps #10 beading needle. Securely tack (sew) down the warp cords (see Fig. 16) to the back of the piece. Make the stitches invisible at the front by sewing in the "ditch" between the first 18g. segment and the 20g. wire. Cut off the excess cord close to the stitching.

3. Sew on a few beads to the front center of the earring to embellish it. Locate the stitches in the "ditches" on both sides of the 20g. wire and position the beads in the center (see Fig. 17). Apply a coat of clear nail polish over the stitches and cord at the center/back of the earring.

Project Three

4. Thread beads onto the bottom part of the 20g. wire. Below the last bead, trim the wire to ⅜" (see Fig. 18).

5. Make sure that the top eyepin loop is on a flat plane with the earring. Bend the 20g. wire straight to the back at a 90° angle below the bottom bead. Make a tight spiral, curling the wire towards the front. (see Fig. 19).

6. Attach an earring wire to the eyepin loop (see Fig. 19).

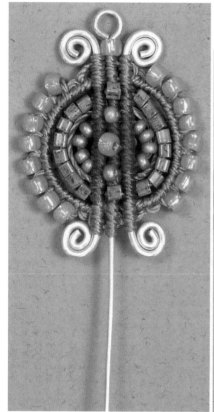

Fig. 17

Fig. 18

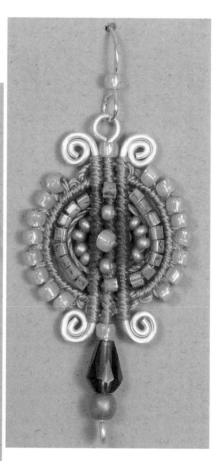

Fig. 19

These long and elegant earrings are my micro-macramé version of the popular Chandelier style. As you can see by the examples here, they lend themselves to different looks depending on your bead and color choices.

Knotted Chandeliers

Materials

Wire:
- (7.5") 18 gauge round wire
- (7") 22 gauge round wire

Cord:
- 18g. Nylon Cord - 12 lengths @ 20" (May be all one color or up to 5 different colors)

Beads (the following were used in the project, others may be substituted):
- (2) 11-12 mm crystal teardrops
- (2) 5 mm crystal rondelles
- (4) 8 mm glass ovals
- (4) 4 mm round crystal or fire polish
- (2) 5 mm metal spacers
- (12) 3 mm metal spacers
- (24) 11° bronze seed beads

Other:
- (2) Earring wires
- #10 sharps beading needle and thread
- Ultra-suede or pig suede (1" X .5")

Project Four

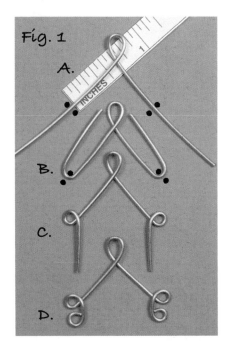

Fig. 1

A.

B.

C.

D.

Part 1 - Shaping the Wire Forms

I recommend that you make the two forms simultaneously. This will help to make them a good match.

1. Cut a 3.75" piece of 18g. wire. Grasp it in the middle with roundnose pliers. Position it approximately $\frac{1}{16}$" from the tips of the pliers.

2. Hold firmly and pinch the wire around the tip forming a "U" shape. Cross the wire ends over each other and move them towards the opposite sides to form a 90° angle with the "legs" (see Fig. 1a).

3. Measure $\frac{5}{8}$" from the bottom of the loop down the wire (see Fig. 1a). This measurement is important, so make sure you measure carefully. It needs to be exactly the same on both sides. The dots show where to place your plier tips.

4. Grasp the wire firmly with round nose pliers at the $\frac{5}{8}$" mark, positioning the wire approximately $\frac{1}{16}$" from the tips of the pliers. Keeping the pliers stationary, wrap the wire around the outer tip and upwards, to form a "U" shape (see Fig. 1b).

5. Reposition the plier tips so that they grasp the wire at the bottom and center of the "U" (see Fig. 1b). Holding the pliers stationary, bring the wire around towards the center and then straight downward (see Fig. 1c).

6. Repeat Steps #4 & 5 on the other "leg". The loop should cross itself on the same side (to the front) as on the opposite leg (see Fig. 1c).

7. Curl the remaining wire tip up in a spiral, positioning the wire approx. $\frac{1}{4}$" from the tips of the pliers (see Fig. 1d). Flatten the form with a hammer if desired (see Fig. 2).

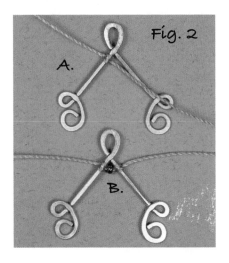

Fig. 2

A.

B.

Part 2 - Adding the Cords and Knotwork

1. Row 1 - Pin the wire form to the board. Find the center point of one cord and tape the cord into place to the left of the form. Make a **VDHH** (Vertical Double Half Hitch) around the left hand leg of wire, below the top loop (see Fig. 2a).

2. Thread a seed bead onto the cord (to the right of the **VDHH**) and push it to the left next to the **VDHH** (see Fig. 2b).

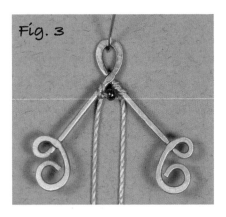

Fig. 3

3. Make a **VDHH** around the right hand leg of the wire (see Fig. 2b). Bring the two tails of the cord to the back and then downward vertically (see Fig. 3). These cords now become vertical warp cords that will be used in the next row.

4. Row 2 - Take another cord, center it, and make a **VDHH** around the left hand leg of the wire, just below Row 1. Make **VDHH**s around the two warp cords (see Fig. 4).

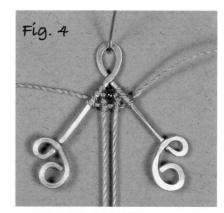

Fig. 4

5. Make a **VDHH** around the right hand leg of the wire (see Fig. 4). Bring the two outer tails of the cord behind the wire and then downward vertically. These cords now become warp cords and are positioned to the outside of the other two warp cords (see Fig. 5).

6. Row 3 - Take another cord and make a **VDHH** around the left hand leg of the wire, just below Row 2. Make a **DHH** (horizontal **DHH**) with the first warp cord (see Fig. 6).

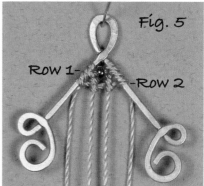

Fig. 5

Row 1- -Row 2

7. Make a **VDHH** around the second warp cord, thread a seed bead onto the cord, then make a **VDHH** around the third warp cord (the bead will sit between the 2 **VDHH**s). Make a **DHH** with the fourth warp cord (see Fig. 6).

8. Make a **VDHH** around the right hand leg of the wire. Bring the two outer tails of the cord downward vertically. These cords now become warp cords and are positioned to the outside of the other four warp cords.

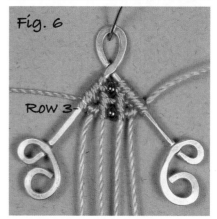

Fig. 6

Row 3-

9. Row 4 - Take another cord and make a **VDHH** around the left hand leg of the wire, just below Row 3. Make **DHH**s with Cords #1 & 2. Make **VDHH**s around the Cords #3 & 4. Make **DHH**s with Cords #5 & 6. (Fig. 7 shows Rows 4 & 5).

10. Make a **VDHH** around the right hand leg of the wire. Bring the two outer tails of the cord behind the wire and downward vertically. These cords now become warp cords and are positioned to the outside of the other six warp cords.

11. Row 5 - Take another cord and make a **VDHH** around the left hand leg of the wire, just below Row 4. Make **DHH**s with Cords #1, 2, & 3.

12. Make a **VDHH** around the Cord #4, thread a seed bead onto the cord, then make a **VDHH** around Cord #5. Make **DHH**s with Cords #6, 7, & 8. Make a **VDHH** around the right hand leg of the wire (see Fig. 7).

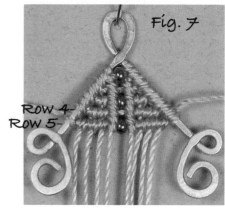

Fig. 7

Row 4-
Row 5-

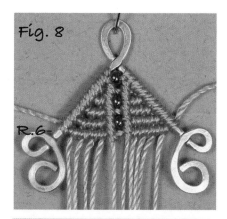

Fig. 8

R.6 -

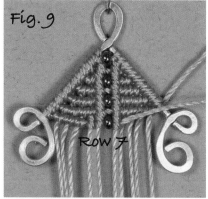

Fig. 9

Row 7

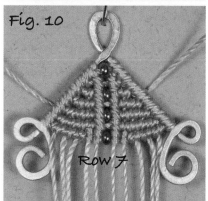

Fig. 10

Row 7

13. Row 6 - Take another cord and make a **VDHH** around the left hand leg of the wire, just below Row 5. Make **DHH**s with Cords #1, 2, 3, & 4.

14. Make **VDHH**s around the Cords #5 & 6. Make **DHH**s with Cords #7, 8, 9, & 10. Make a **VDHH** around the right hand leg of the wire (see Fig. 8).

15. Row 7 (left side) - No new cord is added to this row. Bring the left hand outer tail from Row 6 down behind the wire. Make a **DHH** around the wire (a single **HH** is OK if you are running out of room). This cord will now be used as the **RC** (Runner Cord) for the left side of Row 7.

16. Make **DHH**s with Cords #1, 2, & 3. Make **VDHH**s around Cords #4 & 5. Thread a seed bead onto the **RC** and push it to the left. Make a **VDHH** around Cord #6 (see Fig. 9). Stop here and bring the **RC** behind the remaining warp cords and off to the right.

17. Row 7 (right side) - Bring the outer right hand tail of cord from Row 6 down behind the wire and make a **DHH** around the wire. This cord will serve as the **RC** for the right side of Row 7.

18. Working from right to left, make **DHH**s with Cords #10, 9, & 8. Make a **VDHH** around Cord #7 (see Fig. 10). Bring the **RC** to the back behind the warp cords and off to the left. The **RC**s from Row 7 will no longer be used.

19. Row 8 (left side) - Take Cord #1 and use it as the **RC** for the left side. Make **VDHH**s around Cds #2 - 6 (see Fig. 11). Stop here and bring the **RC** to the back behind the remaining warp cords.

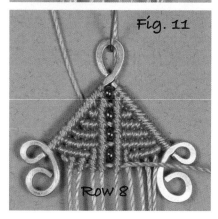

Fig. 11

Row 8

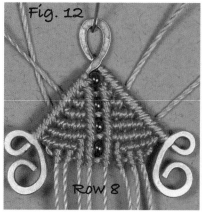

Fig. 12

Row 8

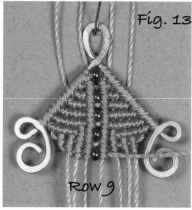

Fig. 13

Row 9

20. Row 8 (right side) - Take Cord #10 and use it as the **RC** for the right side. Working from right to left, make **VDHH**s around Cds #9, 8, & 7 (see Fig. 12). Bring the **RC** to the back behind the remaining warp cords. The **RC**s from Row 8 will no longer be used.

21. Row 9 (left side) - Take Cord #1 and use it as the **RC** for the left side. Make **VDHH**s around Cds #2, 3, & 4. Thread a seed bead onto the **RC**. Make a **VDHH** around Cd #5 (see Fig. 13). Stop here and bring the **RC** to the back behind the remaining warp cords.

22. Row 9 (right side) - Take Cord #8 and use it as the **RC** for the right side. Working from right to left, make **VDHH**s around Cds #7 & 6 (see Fig. 14). Bring the **RC** to the back behind the remaining warp cords. The **RC**s from Row 9 will no longer be used.

23. Row 10 (left side) - Take Cord #1 and use it as the **RC** for the left side. Make **VDHH**s around Cds #2, 3 & 4 (see Fig. 15). Stop and bring the **RC** to the back behind the remaining warp cords.

24. Row 10 (right side) - Take Cord #6 and use it as the **RC** for the right side. Working from right to left, make a **VDHH** around Cd #5 (see Fig. 15). Bring the **RC** to the back behind the remaining warp cords. The **RC**s from Row 10 will no longer be used.

25. Row 11 - Take Cd #1 and make a **VDHH** around Cd #2. Take Cd #4 and make a **VDHH** around Cd #3 (see Fig. 16). Bring Cds #1 and #4 to the back of the piece.

Part 3 - Adding the Fringe and Finishing

1. Lining for the back of the earrings: Cut 2 pieces of suede or ultra suede approx. $\frac{1}{2}$" X $\frac{1}{2}$" each. Trim if necessary to fit. Snip off a tiny bit from each corner to soften the shape a little. Set them aside for now (Fig. 17b shows the liner size and placement).

2. Flip the earring to the back and cut off all of the cords to approx. $\frac{1}{4}$". **Do Not** cut off the 2 center hanging cords!!! (see Fig. 17a).

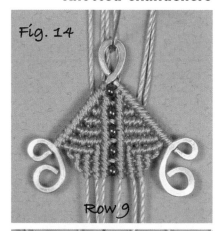
Fig. 14
Row 9

Fig. 15
Row 10

Fig. 16
Row 11

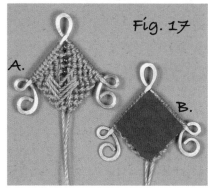
Fig. 17
A.
B.

Project Four

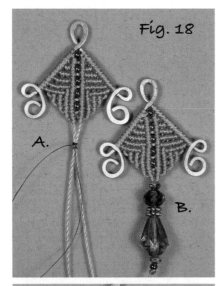

Fig. 18

A.

B.

Fig. 19

Fig. 20

3. Flip the earring to the front. Join the 2 hanging cords together by wrapping them tightly together with beading thread approx. $\frac{1}{4}$" from the top (see Fig. 18a). Wrap a few times to secure them. Tie off the thread. Add a dab of clear nail polish. **Note** - If your beads are a very tight fit on the cords, make sure they fit over the thread before adding nail polish.

4. Thread the center fringe beads onto the 2 joined cords. Cut off one of the cords flush with the bottom of the last bead. Add a seed bead and tie off the cord with an Overhand Knot. Add a dab of clear nail polish and let dry. Cut off the excess cord below the knot (see Fig. 18b).

5. Next, attach the 2 sewn-on fringe segments adjacent to the center fringe. Use a beading needle and about 15" of thread. Knot off the thread at one end and sew through the fibers at the bottom edge (approximately $\frac{1}{8}$" to the right of center). Add fringe beads with a stopper seed bead at the end. Pass the needle back up through the fringe beads, bypassing the stopper bead, sewing through the fibers at the bottom edge once again. Repeat on the left side (see Fig. 19).

6. Glue the lining in place with tacky glue, hiding any tails of cord and thread behind it. Sew the lining to the knotting around the edges if desired.

7. Cut 4 lengths of 22g. wire @ 1.5" to 1.75" each (depending on the length of your outer fringe segments). Make a small tight spiral on one end. Kink the wire straight up from the spiral. Repeat with the other 3 wires. **Note** - since the length is variable, you may want to experiment with brass or copper first if using a more expensive wire.

8. Arrange your chosen fringe beads onto the wires. Above the top bead, bend the wire at a 90° angle perpendicular to the plane of the spiral. Cut to approximately $\frac{1}{4}$" and make a loop to the back with round nose pliers. Repeat with the other 3 segments. **Note** - the spirals should face outwards on each side.

9. Attach the outer wire fringe segments on each side. Attach an earring wire to the top loop.

MM Classic Charm Bracelet

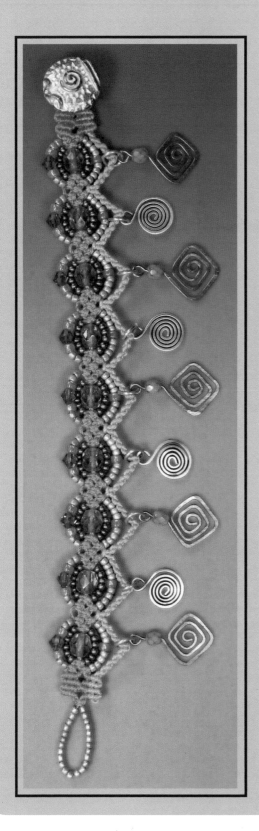

My micro-macrame charm bracelet is a new twist on a popular style. The band has a classic micro-macrame beaded motif which is bordered by an attractive Double Half Hitch chain suspending the wirework charms.

Materials

Wire:
- (17.5") 20g. round Copper wire
- (14") 20g. round Sterling Silver wire

18g. Nylon cord:
- (3) lengths @ 60" Color A
- (1) length @ 80" Color B

Beads:
The following beads were used in the example, others may be substituted if desired.
- 11° seed beads in 2 metallic colors (108 silver and 108 gold matte)
- (9) 6 mm round fire polish
- (9) 4 mm crystal bicones
- (20+) 8° seed beads

Other:
- (9) 5 - 6 mm jump rings
- (1) Button (5/8")
- #10 Sharps beading needle (or similar)
- 20" or more of Nymo D (or similar) in matching color to the cord

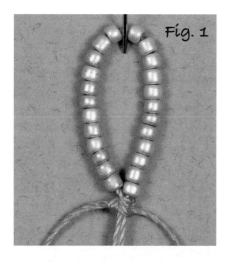

Fig. 1

Part I - The Knotted Band

1. Thread approximately 1.5" of 11° seed beads onto one of the Color A cords. Form it into a loop and drape it over a pin with the two cords hanging downward (see Fig. 1).

2. Take another Color A cord and use it to make a **SQK** around the 2 loop cords (see Fig. 1). Check and see that the loop fits over the button. Adjust the beads if needed.

3. Row 1 - Pin through the **SQK** to hold. Bring the left hand "filler" cord from the **SQK** horizontally to the left and make a **DHH** (Double Half Hitch) around it with the outer left cord. Bring the right hand "filler" cord from the **SQK** horizontally to the right and make a **DHH** around it with the outer right cord (see Fig. 2).

4. Row 1 (cont.) - Attach the remaining Color A cord to the horizontal **AC** (Anchor Cord) on the right with a **MTK** (Mounting Knot). Attach the Color B cord to the horizontal **AC** on the left with a **MTK**. Pin in place (see Fig. 3).

5. Row 2 (left side) - Bring the left hand **AC** back to the right and make a row of 3 **DHH**s, stopping at the center of the band. Row 2 (right side) - Bring the right hand **AC** back to the left and make a row of 3 **DHH**s, stopping at the center of the band (see Fig. 4).

6. Join the two **AC**s at the center by crossing the left hand **AC** over the right, then bringing it under and back to the left horizontally. Bring the right hand **AC** to the right horizontally.

7. Row 3 (both sides) - Working from the center out to the sides, make 3 **DHH**s on each side (see Fig. 5).

8. Row 4 (both sides) - Working from the sides to the center, make 3 **DHH**s on each side (see Fig. 6).

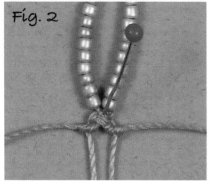

Fig. 2

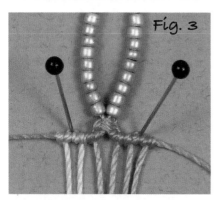

Fig. 3

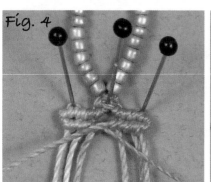

Fig. 4

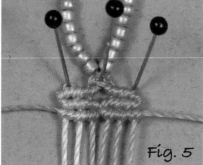

Fig. 5

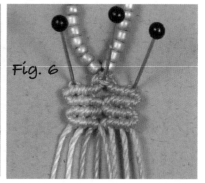

Fig. 6

Note - I will now refer to the cords as #1 - 8, according to their sequence from left to right.

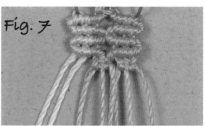

Fig. 7

9. **Beaded Motif** - Make a **SQK** (Square Knot) with Cds #3 - 5. There will only be one "filler" cord (Cd #4). Make a **SQK** with Cds #6 - 8. There will only be one "filler" cord (Cd #7) (see Fig. 7).

10. Make a **SQK** with Cds #4 - 7. There will be two "filler" cords (Cds #5 & 6). Thread a 6 mm bead onto Cds #5 & 6 (see Fig. 8).

Fig. 8

11. Thread approximately 6 seed beads on both Cd #4 and Cd #7. Make another **SQK** with Cds #4 - 7 below the 6 mm bead (see Fig. 8).

12. Thread beads onto Cd #3 (for example - (4) 11°,(1) 8°, (4) 11°). Make a **SQK** with Cds # 3 - 5 (see Fig. 9).

Fig. 9

13. Thread beads onto Cd #8 (for example - (2) 11°, (1) 8°, (1) 4 mm bicone, (1) 8°, (2) 11°). Make a **SQK** with Cds #6 - 8 (see Fig. 9).

14. Make a **SQK** with Cds #4 - 7 (see Fig. 10).

15. **Zigzag Chain** - Bring Cd #2 horizontally to the left. Make a **DHH** around it with Cd #1 (Note that the cords will switch position when you do this). Repeat 4 times. The chain will make an angle to the left (see Fig. 11).

Fig. 10

16. Place a pin in the board just to the left of Cd #2. Bring Cd #1 below the pin and horizontally to the right. Make a **DHH** around it with Cd #2. Repeat 4 times. The chain will make an angle back to the right (see Fig. 12).

17. Use Cd #2 to make a **LHK** (Larks Head Knot) around Cd #3 (see Fig. 13).

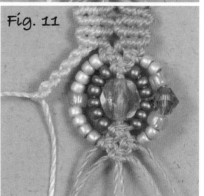

Fig. 11

Fig. 13

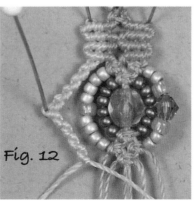

Fig. 12

Fig. 14

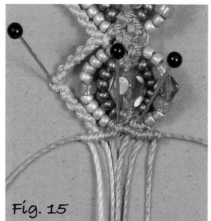

Fig. 15

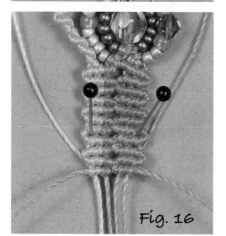

Fig. 16

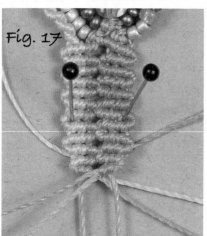

Fig. 17

18. Repeat Steps #9 - 17 eight times omitting Step 17 in the last set (see Fig. 14).

19. The Bottom Tab - Pin the bottom 2 **SQK**s and the adjoining chain to the board in an even horizontal row. Take Cd #4 and bring it horizontally to the left. Use it as the **AC** for the left half of the band and make **DHH**s with Cds #3, 2, & 1 (see Fig. 15).

20. Take Cd #5 and bring it horizontally to the right. Use it as the **AC** for the right half of the band and make **DHH**s with Cds #6, 7, & 8 (see Fig. 15).

21. Next row (left side) - Bring the left hand **AC** back to the right and make a row of 3 **DHH**s, stopping at the center of the band. Next row (right side) - Bring the right hand **AC** back to the left and make a row of 3 **DHH**s, stopping at the center of the band (see Fig. 16).

22. Join the two **AC**s at the center by crossing the left hand **AC** over the right, then bringing it under and back to the left horizontally. Bring the right hand **AC** to the right horizontally.

23. Next row (both sides) - Working from the center out to the sides, make 3 **DHH**s on each side (see Fig. 16).

24. Repeat the previous Steps (21 -23) to make the tab long enough so that the top beaded loop overlaps the tab when the bracelet is wrapped around your wrist. Go on to the next step when the band (measured from the bottom of the beaded loop) is approx. 3/8" shorter than your wrist measurement.

25. If the two **AC**s are at the sides, make another row to bring them both back to the center, if they are at the center already, go to the next step.

26. Bring the left hand **AC** horizontally to the left and make a **DHH** with Cd #3. Omitting Cd #2 from knotting, skip to Cd #1 and make another **DHH** (see Fig. 16).

27. Bring the right hand **AC** horizontally to the right and make a **DHH** with Cd #6. Omitting Cd #7 from knotting, skip to Cd #8 and make another **DHH** (see Fig. 16). Bring Cds #2 and #7 to the back and out of the way (see Fig. 16).

28. Next row (left side) - Bring the left hand **AC** and Cd #1 (treating them like a single unit) back to the right horizontally. Make a **DHH** with the remaining left hand warp cord (see Fig. 17).

29. Next row (right side) - Bring the right hand **AC** and the farthest right hand warp cord (treating them like a single unit) back to the left horizontally. Make a **DHH** with the remaining right hand warp cord (see Fig. 17).

30. Make a hem with the warp cords, bring them to the back of the tab. Sew them down securely with matching beading thread. Cut off the excess cord. Apply some clear nail polish and let dry (see Fig. 18).

31. Sew the button to the center or lower part of the tab, fitting it to your wrist to check proper placement (see Figs. 18a & b).

32. Attach the spiral charms to the nine chain sections with jump rings, alternating the copper charms and the silver charms (see project picture on page 29).

Part 2 - Shaping the Charms

Rounded Spiral (Fig. 19) - **A**. Cut a 3.5" length of 20g. wire and make a small loop on one end. Tightly curl the wire around the loop, leaving approx. ³⁄₈" of straight wire at the end. **B**. Make a small loop facing the opposite way. **C**. Flatten with a chasing hammer, if desired.

Angular Spiral with Bead (Fig. 20) - **A**. Cut a 4" length of 20g. wire and make an unclosed loop on one end leaving room for the chain nose plier tips between the end of the loop and the adjacent wire. **B**. Grasp the wire with the pliers in that space (the dots show plier's tip placement). Bend the wire around the plier's tip at a 90° angle. **C,D,E,F.** Make more 90° bends at the corners until there are 10 corners. **F**. Grasp the remaining wire at the top center and kink the wire straight up. **G**. Add a bead and trim the wire to ³⁄₈". Bend it to the side just above the bead. **H**. Make a loop with your round nose pliers.

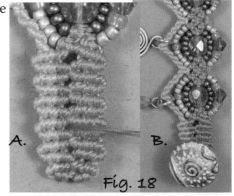

Fig. 18

A.   B.

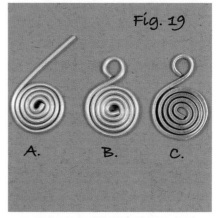

Fig. 19

A.   B.   C.

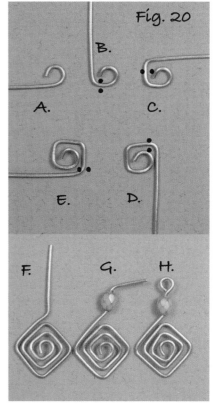

Fig. 20

B.

A.   C.

E.   D.

F.   G.   H.

Blossom Bracelet

This bracelet has a lovely knotted and beaded band that makes a great base for a centerpiece. In this piece it's a "blossom" made of shaped wire and beads. The band also features a unique wirework clasp.

Materials

Wire:
- (20") 18g. round wire
- (13.5") 20g. round wire
- (1.5") 24g. round wire (optional)
- (20") 28g. wire (Fireline may be substituted)

18g Nylon cord:
- (5) lengths @ 74" Color A
- (5) lengths @ 74" Color B

Beads:
The following beads were used in the example, others may be substituted if desired.
- (96+) 4 mm round fire polish
- (20+) 8° seed beads
- (1) 10 mm flat rondelle

Other supplies:
- #10 Sharps beading needle (or similar)
- 80" or more of Nymo D (or similar) in matching color to the cord
- 30 - 50" 6 lb. Fireline (or similar) in complimentary color to the cord

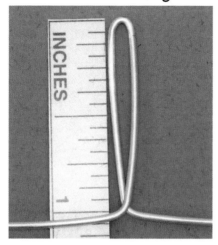

Fig. 1

Fig. 2

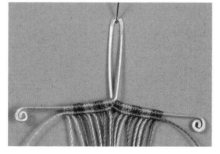

Fig. 3

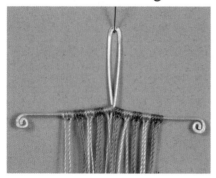

Fig. 4

Part 1 - Forming the Wire Hook & Eye Clasp/End Pieces

1. **Hook Segment** - Cut a 5.5" length of 18g. wire. Grasp it at the center with the tips (narrowest part) of the round nose pliers and bend the ends together.

2. Measure 1" from the bend and make a 90° bend in the left hand wire, bringing it straight out to the right. Measure 1" from the bend and make a 90° bend in the right hand wire, bringing it straight out to the left. The two wires will cross over each other at the middle (see Fig. 1).

3. Make tight downward facing spirals on both ends, gradually curling them inward until the horizontal bottom of the piece is 2.5" wide (see Fig. 3).

4. **Eye Segment** - Cut a 4.25" length of 18g. wire. Grasp it at the center with the widest part of the roundnose pliers. Wrap the ends around the jaw so they cross each other, and bring them straight out to the sides in opposite directions.

5. Make tight downward facing spirals on both ends, gradually curling them inward until the bottom of the piece is 2.5" wide (see Fig. 2).

6. Optional - Lightly flatten the spirals (only) on both pieces, leaving all other wire as is.

Part 2 - The Knotted Band

1. Row 1 - Attach the 10 doubled cords to the "Hook" segment with **MTKs** (Mounting Knots), alternating the colors. I will refer to the 20 vertical cords as Cds #1 - 20 according to their sequence from left to right (see Fig. 3).

2. Row 2 (left side) - Make a single Half Hitch with Cd #11 around Cd #10. Bring Cd #10 horizontally to the left and use it as the **AC** (Anchor Cord) for the left half of Row 2. Working from center to the left, make **DHH**s around the **AC** with Cds #9, 8, 7, and so on across the row (see Fig. 4).

3. Row 2 (right side) - Bring Cd #11 horizontally to the right and use it as the **AC** for the right half of Row 2. Working to the right, make **DHH**s around the **AC** with Cds #12, 13, 14 and so on across the row (see Fig. 4).

Project Six

4. Row 3 (left side) - bring the **AC** back to the right and make a horizontal row of **DHH**s with Cds #1 - 9. Row 3 (right side) bring the **AC** back to the left and make a horizontal row of **DHH**s with Cds #20 - 12. The two **AC**s are now at the center of the band and in their original positions as Cds #10 & #11 (see Fig. 5).

5. On each of the sides, grasp the wire with the top edge of flat nose or chain nose pliers next to the outside edge of knots. Bend the wires up and inward towards the center. Adjust the spirals if necessary to fit (see Fig. 6).

6. Row 4 - Group together Cds #1 & 2, treating them as a single unit. Group together Cds #3 & 4 treating them as a single unit. Make a short **AHHch** (Alternating Half Hitch Chain) starting by making a **HH** with Cds #3 - 4 around Cds #1 - 2. Next make a **HH** with Cds #1 - 2 around Cds #3 - 4. Finally, make a **HH** with Cds #3 - 4 around Cds #1 - 2 (see Fig. 6).

7. Move to the right and make the same kind of **AHHch** with (Cds # 5 - 6 and #7 - 8), (Cds # 9 - 10 and #11 - 12), (Cds #13 - 14 and #15 - 16), and (Cds #17 - 18 and #19 - 20) (see Fig. 6).

8. Row 5 - Make a **SQK** (Square Knot) with Cds #3 - 6. Cds #3 & 6 will be the **KC**s (Knotting Cords) and Cds #4 & 5 will be the filler cords. Move to the right and make a **SQK**s with Cds #7 - 10, Cds #11 - 14, and Cds #15 - 18. You will have a total of 4 **SQK**s in the row. Cds #1 & 2 and Cds #19 & 20 will remain unknotted (see Fig. 7).

9. Rows 6 through 52 (may be more or less) - Repeat Steps 6 - 8 until the knotted part of the band is ½" shorter than your wrist measurement (or the preferred size of the bracelet). For example, if the circumference of my wrist is 7", I will stop making rows at 6.5". Make the final row a row of **AHH** chains (as in Steps 6 & 7) if possible (see Fig. 8).

Tip - The piece will tend to get narrower as you complete a few rows. Pull outward on the edges periodically and pin them in place to maintain a wider width.

Fig. 5

Fig. 6

Fig. 7

Fig. 8

Micro-Macramé and Wire Jewelry

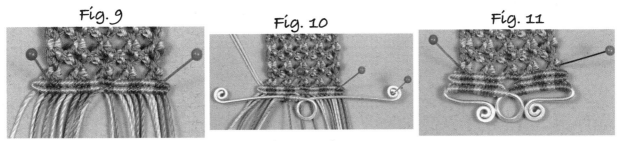

Fig. 9   *Fig. 10*   *Fig. 11*

10. Rows 53 & 54 - Repeat Steps #2, 3, & 4 (see Fig. 9).

11. Row 55 - Attach the cords to the "Eye" segment of the clasp with **DHH**s (see Fig. 10 - 11).

12. Make a hem, bringing the cords to the back and sew them down securely. Make the stitches invisible from the front by sewing in the "ditch" between the last two rows. Apply a dab of clear nail polish and let dry. Cut off the excess cords.

13. On both sides, grasp the wire with the top edge of the flat or chain nose pliers next to the outside edge of knots. Bend the wires inward towards the center. Adjust the spirals if necessary to fit (see Fig. 11).

Part 3 - Embellishing the Netted Band

1. Attach a beading needle to an 80" length of sturdy beading thread. Double the thread and knot it off with an **OVK**. Optional - coat the thread with beeswax to keep it from tangling.

2. Secure the thread at the back of the piece in Row 3 between the 4th and 5th warp cords. Bring the needle to the front of the band and thread on a 4 mm bead. Push the bead up so it sits on top of the knotted netting (see Fig. 12).

3. Working from top to bottom, sew down through the center of the first **SQK** in Row 5. Add a bead, sew through the next **SQK** down (Row 7). Continue the same pattern down the entire length of the left side of the bracelet. Each of the beads will sit in a space between **SQK**s.

4. Sew through the back of the bottom horizontal row of **DHH**s to secure the thread at the end of the vertical row. Come back up in the opposite direction and add beads to the next vertical row to the right. Leave 2 or 3 centermost "spaces" unbeaded (you will attach the centerpiece here), then complete the upper half of the row (see Fig. 12).

5. Sew through the back of Row 3 to secure the thread at the top of the vertical row. Come back down in the opposite direction and add beads to the next vertical row to the right. Leave 2 or 3 centermost "spaces" unbeaded, then complete the lower half of the row.

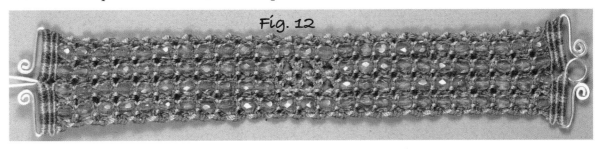

Fig. 12

Project Six

6. Sew through the back of the bottom horizontal row of **DHH**s to secure the thread at the end of the row. Come back up in the opposite direction and add beads to the last vertical row on the right. Secure and knot off the thread at the back of Row 3.

Part 4 - Forming the Wire and Bead Blossom

1. Outer "Petals": Cut a 10" length of 18 gauge wire. Using the top edge of flat nose pliers, make a 90° bend 1" from one end. Make a second 90° bend $\frac{3}{8}$" from the first (see Fig. 13).

2. Make a sharp bend at $\frac{1}{2}$" bringing the wire back in the opposite direction (see Fig. 14).

3. Continue forming petal shapes with $\frac{1}{2}$" sides and a $\frac{3}{8}$" outer edges until there are a total of 6 petals (see Fig. 15).

4. Trim each of the ends of the wire to $\frac{7}{8}$". With the tips of chain nose pliers, make very small outward facing loops. Compress them with the pliers to flatten the roundness a bit. Flatten the outer edges of the petals (see Fig. 15).

5. Inner "Petals": Cut a 13.5" length of 20 gauge wire. Make a sharp bend at $\frac{5}{8}$" from one end bringing the wire back to the right. Make a sharp bend at $\frac{3}{8}$" and bring the wire back to the left. Make a sharp bend at $\frac{3}{8}$" and bring the wire back to the right (see Fig. 16).

6. Make a sharp bend at $\frac{1}{2}$" and bring the wire back to the left. Make a sharp bend at $\frac{1}{2}$" and bring the wire back to the right (see Fig. 17).

7. Repeat Steps # 6 & 7 until there are 13 points on the left outside edge. This side will maintain an even edge, while the other side will have an uneven edge (see Fig. 18).

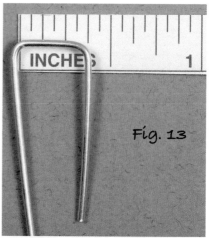

Fig. 13

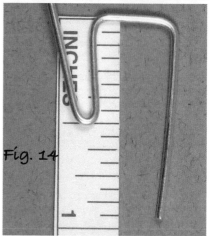

Fig. 14

Fig. 15

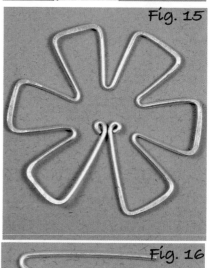

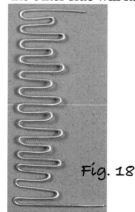

Fig. 18

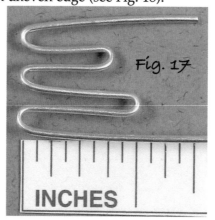

Fig. 17

Fig. 16

Fig. 19

Fig. 20

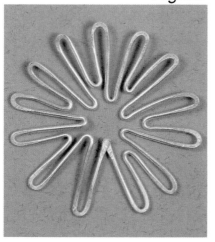

Fig. 21

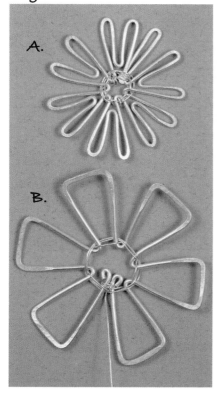

A.

B.

8. Flatten the tips of the points on the even edge only, not on the uneven edge. Trim the wire on both ends to ½" and flatten the tips, being careful not to flatten any adjacent wire (see Fig. 19).

9. Spread apart the outer (even) tips and pinch together the inner (uneven tips) to form a rounded shape (see Fig. 20).

10. Line up the two flattened wire ends, overlapping them at the tips. Take a 20" length of 28g. wire (Fireline may be substituted in a pinch) and secure one end of it to the piece by wrapping it around the tips 2 or 3 times.

11. Weave the 28g. wire over and under the 6 longest inside bends only, pulling them together as closely and neatly as possible. Weave around the piece about 3 times, encasing the wire ends as you go. All of the outer edge tips should be evenly spaced. Secure the 28g. wire with a few wraps and cut it off (see Fig. 21a).

12. Take the Outer Petals wire form and line up the two looped wire ends side by side. Take the remainder of the 28g. wire and secure one end of it to the piece by wrapping it around the wire next to the loops 2 or 3 times (see Fig. 21b).

13. Weave the 28g. wire over and under the 5 inside bends leaving them slightly spread apart at the base. Weave around the piece about 3 times, encasing the wire ends as you go. The outer edge "petals" should be evenly spaced. Secure the 28g. wire with a few wraps but don't cut it off.

14. Place the smaller wire form on top of the "Outer Petals" form, positioning the 28g. wire to come up in the bend of one of the longer inner points of the smaller form. Cross the wire over the piece to the opposite inner bend, then under the piece coming up at the next bend, rotating the piece and using all of the inner bends of the smaller form as the anchor points. You'll only need to do about 4 or 5 complete wraps to hold them together.

15. Wrap the 28g. wire a few times to secure it and cut off any excess.

16. Cut a 30" piece of Fireline, thread it onto a beading needle, double it and knot it off. Sew the wire forms securely to the center of the bracelet (see Fig. 22).

Project Six

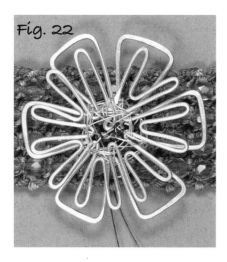

Fig. 22

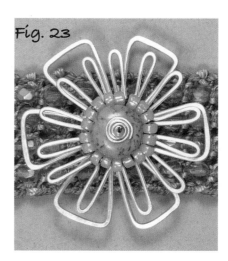

Fig. 23

17. Optional - Make a tight spiral with 1.5" of 24g. wire to place on top of the rondelle bead (see Fig. 23).

18. Sew up through the middle of the piece and thread on the rondelle, spiral, and a stopper bead. Sew back down through the beads to the back (bypassing the stopper). Sew back up and back a second time for extra security (see Fig. 23).

19. Add a row of 8° beads around the rondelle and "couch" them with thread several times around the ring to hold them in place. Bring the remaining thread to the back of the piece and knot it off (see Fig. 23).

20. Finishing the Clasp - Bend the center part of the "Hook" clasp segment to the back at the halfway point (measure on your wrist to check first) to form a hook (see Figures 24 & 25).

Fig. 24

Fig. 25

Nefertitti Cuff

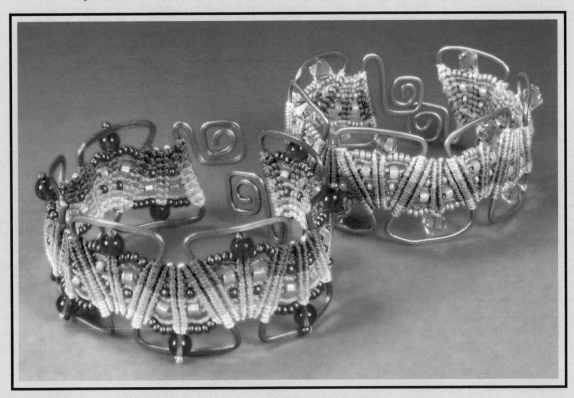

Materials

Wire:
- (30") 16g. round wire

18g. Nylon cord:
- (5) lengths @ 80" of 5 different colors

Beads:
The following beads were used in the example, others may be substituted if desired.
- (12) Accent beads - 4 mm rounds, drops or similar
- (96+) 11° seed beads
- (24) 8° seed beads

Other:
- Beading or fine sewing needle and thread in complimentary color
- Ruler (flat metal preferred)

This handsome cuff looks especially good when the cord colors graduate from dark to light shades. Using mostly Double Half Hitches, the pattern repeats and is not as complex as it looks. And no clasp is needed, so one size fits all.

Project Seven

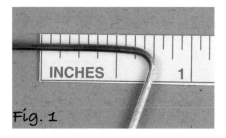

Fig. 1

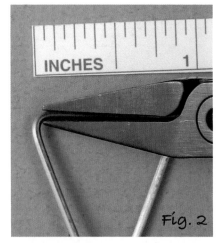

Fig. 2

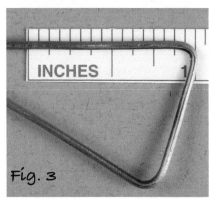

Fig. 3

Part I - Forming the Wire

1. Locate the center point on the 30" wire (at 15"). Grasp the wire $\frac{3}{8}$" to one side of the center with the tips of your flat nose pliers and bend it in at a 30° angle (see Fig. 1).

2. Measure $\frac{3}{4}$" from the first bend and make another 30° bend towards the inside, creating a small flat section of wire approx. $\frac{3}{4}$" long (see Fig. 1 & 2).

3. On one side, measure 1" from the flat $\frac{3}{4}$" section and bend the wire outwards parallel to the $\frac{3}{4}$" section (see Fig. 3 & 4). Repeat Step #2, bending the wire back towards the opposite side, creating another $\frac{3}{4}$" section of wire parallel to the first one (see Fig. 5). Repeat on the other side.

Note - the measurements don't need to be exact, however you do need to be consistent and use the same measuring and bending method every time to achieve a uniform look.

4. Continue to work from the center of the bracelet out towards the ends. Alternate from side to side until you have (12) $\frac{3}{4}$" flat sections completed, 6 on each outer edge of the bracelet (see Fig. 6).

5. Cut the remaining ends of the wire to 3.25" each. Bend them back in the opposite direction parallel with the edges (see Figs. 7 & 8).

6. Make loose squared-off spirals on each end (see Fig. 9). Notice that one of the spirals has one more bend than the other (see Fig. 10).

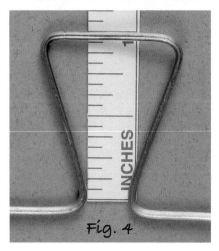

Fig. 4

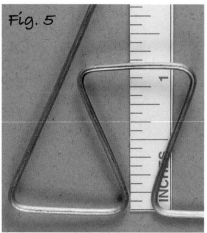

Fig. 5

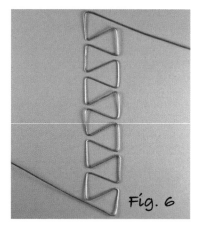

Fig. 6

Wired Micro-Macramé Jewelry

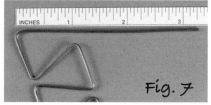

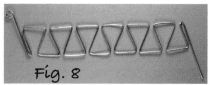

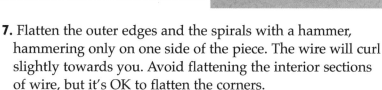

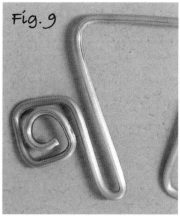

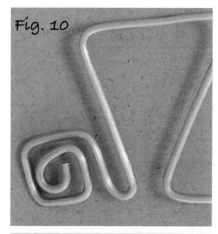

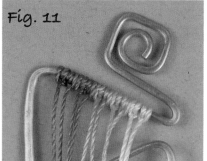

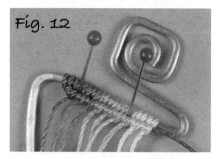

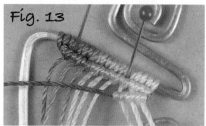

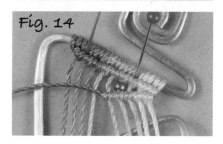

7. Flatten the outer edges and the spirals with a hammer, hammering only on one side of the piece. The wire will curl slightly towards you. Avoid flattening the interior sections of wire, but it's OK to flatten the corners.

Part 2 - The Knotted Sections

Left facing segments -

1. Attach the 5 cords to the wire at one end with **MTK**s (Mounting Knots) (see Fig. 11). Secure the wire to the board with tape to flatten it out and make it easier to handle.

2. Bring the left hand cord to the right just below the row of **MTK**s. This same cord will be used as the **AC** for the left-facing segment (Steps 2 - 14). That will leave 9 warp (vertical) cords to work with and I will refer to them as Cds #1 - 9 according to their sequence from left to right.

3. Working from left to right, make a row of **DHH**s parallel to the row of **MTK**s (see Fig. 12). Bring the AC back around to the left (see Fig. 13).

4. Attach Cds #9, 8, & 7 to the **AC** with **DHH**s keeping the **AC** at a slight angle (see Fig. 13). **Note** - This row will be horizontal (at a right angle to the bracelet's outer edge).

5. Thread an 11° seed bead onto Cd #6 and attach it to the **AC** with a **DHH**. Attach Cd #5 to the **AC** with a **DHH** (see Fig. 14).

Project Seven

Fig. 15

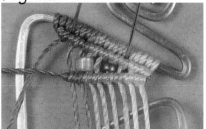

Fig. 16

Fig. 17

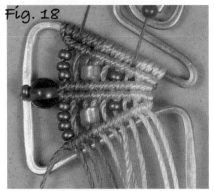

Fig. 18

Fig. 19

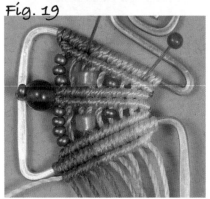

6. Thread an 8° seed bead onto both Cds #4 & 3 (see Fig. 15). If your bead is too narrow to accommodate two cords, leave Cd #4 free and thread the bead onto Cd #3 only. Attach both cords to the **AC** with **DHH**s, making sure that the cord colors remain in the correct order.

7. Attach Cd #2 to the **AC** with a **DHH** (see Fig. 15). Thread (3 or 4, whichever fits) 11° seed beads to Cd #1. Attach it to the **AC** with a **DHH** (see Fig. 16).

8. Thread an accent bead onto the **AC** followed by a stopper bead (see Fig. 17). Thread the cord back through in the opposite direction (bypassing the stopper bead) and adjust the accent bead so that it sits at the end of the knotted row. (With some accent beads such as top-drilled drops, a stopper bead is not required).

9. Make a row of **DHH**s parallel and identical to the previous row, starting with Cd #1 and working left to right (see Fig. 17).

10. Bring the **AC** back around to the left again. This row will be at an angle and parallel to the wire below it (see Fig. 18). Attach Cds #9, 8, & 7 to the **AC** with **DHH**s.

11. Thread an 11° seed bead onto Cd #6 and attach it to the **AC**. Attach Cd #5 to the **AC** (see Fig. 19).

12. Thread an 8° seed bead onto both Cds #4 & 3. Attach both cords to the **AC** (see Fig. 19).

13. Attach Cd #2 to the **AC**. Thread (3 or 4) 11° seed beads to Cd #1. Attach it to the **AC** (see Fig. 19). Bring all of the cords behind the next wire section.

14. Starting with Cd #1 (the **AC** from the previous row) and working from left to right, attach all of the cords to the wire with **DHH**s (see Fig. 19).

Right facing segments -

1. Bring Cd #10 to the left just below the row of **DHH**s. This same cord will be used as the **AC** for the entire right -facing segment. I will refer to the remaining cords as Cds #1 - 9.

2. Working from right to left, make a row of **DHH**s parallel to the row of **DHH**s above it (see Fig. 19). Bring the **AC** back around to the right (see Fig. 20).

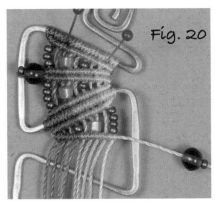
Fig. 20

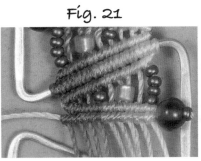
Fig. 21

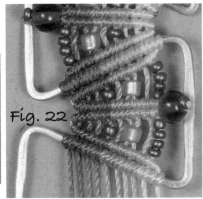
Fig. 22

3. Attach Cds #1, 2, & 3 to the **AC** with **DHH**s. Thread an 11° seed bead onto Cd #4 and attach it to the **AC**. Attach Cd #5 to the **AC** (see Fig. 20).

4. Thread an 8° seed bead onto both Cds #6 & 7. Attach both cords to the **AC** making sure that the cord colors remain in the correct order (see Fig. 20).

5. Attach Cd #8 to the **AC**. Thread (3 or 4) 11° seed beads to Cd # 9. Attach it to the **AC**.

6. Thread an accent bead onto the **AC** followed by a stopper bead (see Fig. 20). Thread the cord back through in the opposite direction (bypassing the stopper bead) and adjust the accent bead so that it sits at the end of the knotted row.

7. Make a row of **DHH**s parallel to and identical to the previous row, starting with Cd #9 and working from right to left (see Fig. 21).

8. Bring the **AC** back around to the right again. This row will be at an angle and parallel to the wire below it. Attach Cds #1, 2, & 3 to the **AC** with **DHH**s (see Fig. 22).

9. Thread an 11° seed bead onto Cd #4 and attach it to the **AC**. Attach Cd #5 to the **AC**.

10. Thread an 8° seed bead onto both Cds #6 & 7. Attach both cords to the **AC** (see Fig. 22).

11. Attach Cd #8 to the **AC** with a **DHH**. Thread (3 or 4) 11° seed beads to Cd #9 and it to the **AC**. Bring all of the cords behind the next wire section.

12. Starting with Cd #10 (the **AC** for the previous row) and working from right to left, attach all of the cords to the wire with **DHH**s (see Fig. 22).

Complete the remainder of the knotted sections, alternating left and right facing segments (see Fig. 23). Do not attach the cords to the bottom wire yet.

Fig. 23

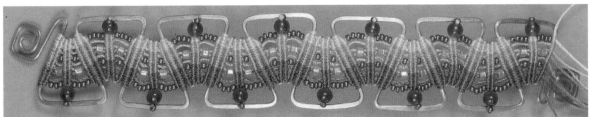

Fig. 24

Part 3 - Finishing

1. Bring all of the cords behind the bottom wire (see Fig. 24). Open up the bend of the lower spiral section a bit to give you more room to work with when attaching the cords.

2. Attach Cd #10 to the wire with a **DHH** (see Fig. 24). Bring Cd #10 to the left and parallel with the wire.

Fig. 25

3. Treating Cd #10 and the wire like a single unit, make a **DHH** around them with Cd #9 (see Fig. 25). Bring the tail of Cd #10 to the back of the piece behind all of the remaining cords. Bring it up and off to the left and tape if needed.

4. Treating Cd #9 and the wire like a single unit, make a **DHH** around them with Cd #8 (see Fig. 26). Bring the tail of Cd #9 to the back of the piece behind all of the remaining cords.

Fig. 26

5. Continue working towards the left and attach all of the remaining cords in the same manner, encasing the previous **DHH** cord and wire together as one unit within the next **DHH**, then bringing it to the back of the piece before moving to the next **DHH** (see Fig. 27). The last cord, Cd #1 will be the only cord that won't be encased along with the wire.

6. Flip the piece to the back. Cut off all of the cords close to the knotting except for Cd #1 & 2 (see Figures 28 & 29).

Fig. 27

7. Tack (sew) down Cds #1 & 2 to the back of the knotting with beading thread. Cut off the excess cord and apply a dab of clear nail polish (see Fig. 30).

8. Shape the cuff by very slightly bending the ¾" sections on the edges of the cuff to the inside. Use your fingers or nylon jaw pliers and work from one end to the other alternating from one edge to the other. Adjust as necessary.

Fig. 28

Fig. 29

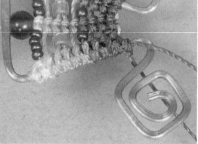

Fig. 30

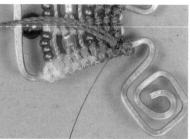

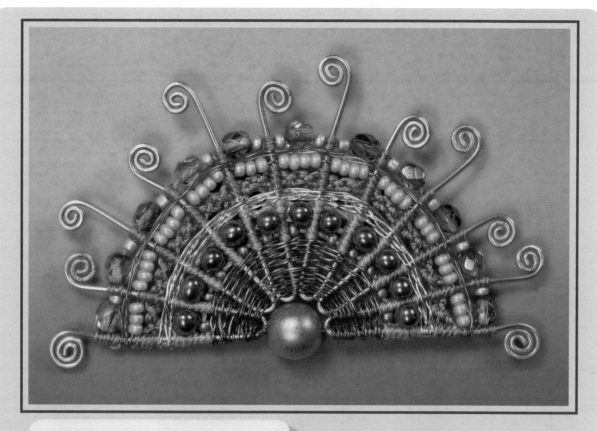

Materials

Wire:
- (24") 20 gauge round wire
- 28 or 30 gauge flexible colored copper wire in different colors:
  - (1) @ 24"
  - (2) @ 20"
  - (1) @ 10"

Cord:
18g. Nylon Cord
- 1 length @ 30"
- 1 length @ 40"

Beads: the following were used in the project, others may be substituted.
- (11) 11° seed beads (Color A)
- (40+) 11° seed beads (Color B)
- (12) 11° seed beads (Color C)
- (11) 4 mm drops
- (11) 4 mm round fire polish
- (1) 8 mm Druk

Other:
- 1" Pin Back
- Narrow sewing needle
- Fray Check

Sunrise Pin

Alternating bands of knotted fiber and twined fine-gauge wire are woven on a wire fan to create this sunny pin. Softly muted cord and shiny wire make an interesting textural contrast.

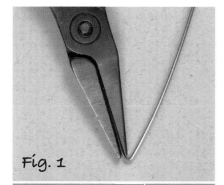

Fig. 1

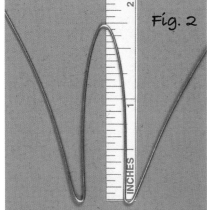

Fig. 2

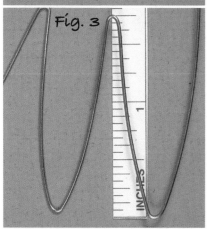

Fig. 3

Fig. 4

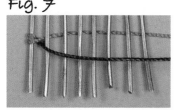

Part 1- Shaping the Wire Base

1. Take the 24" 20g. wire and bend it in half around the tip of round nose pliers (or around one tip of flat nose pliers) making a "softened" angle. If your wire length is curved, bend towards the inside of the curve (see Fig. 1).

2. Place the wire on top of a ruler and measure 1.75" from the tip of the first bend and make opposite bends in each of the spokes, creating a narrow "petal" shape (see Fig. 2).

3. Measure 1.75" on each of the spokes and bend them in the opposite direction, forming the tips of the next petal shapes (see Fig. 3). Working to the left and right, make (2) more petals on the left, and (2) more petals to the right of center for a total of 5 petals. The wire ends should face outward on both sides (see Fig. 4).

Part 2 - Twined Wire, Color Bands 1 & 2

• **Half -Twist Twining** is a basketry technique where 2 "weavers" weave over and under the spokes simultaneously, encasing the spokes. Wire is used in the pin project, cord in the example below. After securing the wire to spoke #1 by wrapping it around once, there will be one Weaver (A) on top of the spoke and one Weaver (B) below the spoke (see Fig. 5). Bring the Weaver A down to the back between spokes #1 & 2 (see Fig. 6). Pass Weaver B under Weaver A and over spoke #2 (see Fig. 7) and then down between spoke #2 & 3 (see Fig. 8). Pass the Weaver A under Weaver B and then up over spoke #3 (see Fig. 8). Then bring Weaver A down between spokes #3 & 4. Pass the Weaver B under it and up over the next spoke and so on (see Fig. 9).

Fig. 5

Fig. 6

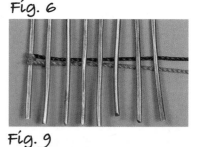

Fig. 7

Fig. 8

Fig. 9

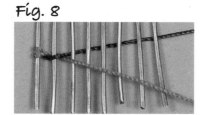

Color Band #1

1. Hold the wire base with the petal tips facing down (see Fig. 4). Locate the center of a 24" length of 28 or 30g. "weaver" wire and secure it to the outer left hand wire spoke by wrapping it around once (see Fig. 10a).

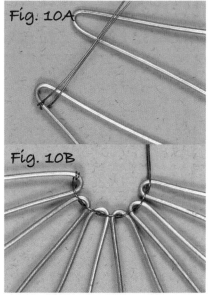

Fig. 10A

2. Twine from left to right to the other side of the form pulling together all of the wire spokes at the base (see Fig. 10b). When you get to the end, flip the wire form over and twine the next row going left to right again.

Note - Treat the two spokes of each "petal" as a single unit when twining this color band. The outer left (single) spoke will be spoke #1, the next two spokes pulled together are spoke #2, the next two joined spokes are spoke #3, and so on. The outer right (single) spoke is spoke #7 (see Fig. 10b).

Fig. 10B

3. Stop when you have completed 6 rows of twining (see Fig. 11). Wrap one of the 28g. weavers around the outer spoke once to secure it. (Leave the other weaver wire for now, it will be used in the next color band). Thread it through towards the center, passing it through the space between the woven wires (see Fig. 12). You can use a narrow needle, if needed.

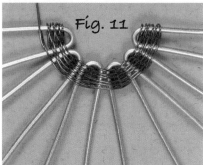

Fig. 11

4. Secure it at the inner bend by wrapping it around the wire twice (see Fig. 12). Thread on an 8 mm bead and push it into position (see Fig. 13).

Fig. 12

5. Wrap the wire around the opposite bend (next to where the wire exits the bead) twice to secure it (see Fig. 13).

6. Pass the wire back through the bead towards the first bend. Wrap the wire around the bend once and then pass it back through the bead towards the second bend. Cut off the excess wire flush where it exits the bead.

Fig. 13

Color Band #2

7. On the same side as the remaining weaver, attach a 20" length of 28 or 30g. wire, wrapping it once around the outer spoke. Pair the leftover weaver from Color Band #1 with one of the new weavers and treat the two as a single unit. This will help soften the transition to the new color, while using up the old weaver.

Fig. 14

8. Working from left to right make a row of twining.

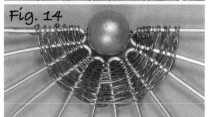

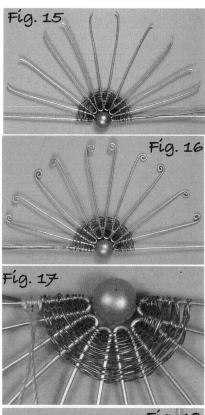

Fig. 15

Fig. 16

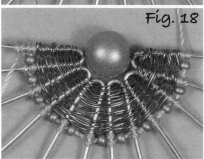

Fig. 17

Fig. 18

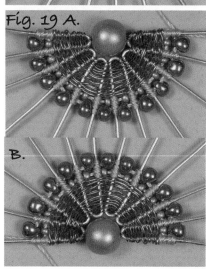

Fig. 19 A.

B.

9. Flip the piece and again twine from left to right, but starting in this row (and from now on), twine around each of the individual 12 spokes (see Fig. 14).

10. The leftover weaver from Color Band #1 will soon be too short to complete another row. When this happens, do the following: To secure and disguise any leftover weavers (from any row), bring them outward and parallel to the outer spoke. When making the subsequent rows, encase the tail(s) along with the outer spokes. After securing the weaver to the spoke, the excess wire or cord is then cut off.

11. Continue twining the Color Band #2 weavers until they become too short to work with (see Fig. 14).

Part 3 - Shaping the Spokes

1. Snip each of the petals at the top/center of the tip with flush cutters. Trim off any beveled ends. Straighten out each spoke (except for the tips) with your fingers and space them evenly (see Fig. 15).

2. Except for the two outer spokes, each of the spoke's tips will curl slightly either left or right. Make small tight spirals in each spoke in the direction of the curl. Just make one or two turns in the spirals for now, you can adjust them later if necessary (see Fig. 16).

Color Band #3

Notes - Although you will have to reposition the piece frequently during assembly the pictures will not always show every position. When I refer to the left and right outer spokes in the directions this is with the big bead to the top (see Fig. 17). The twining is easiest to do while holding the piece, however you will probably want to pin the piece to a board for the knotted segments.

1. Position the wire form with the big bead to the top. Fold a 30" cord so that one half is 4" longer than the other.

2. Positioning the longer half of the cord to the outside, attach the cord to the outer left hand spoke with a **MTK** (Mounting Knot), encasing any leftover weavers (see Fig. 17). Snip off any excess weaver wire flush with the left side of the **MTK** (be careful not to cut into the cord!).

3. Thread an 11° seed bead onto the right hand cord and push it up next to the **MTK**. Make a **DHH** (Double Half Hitch) around the next spoke. Thread on another bead, make a **DHH** around the next spoke. Complete the row in the same way. Encase leftover weavers (if any) along with the outside spoke (see Fig. 18).

Fig. 20

4. Thread a drop bead onto the left hand cord. Make a **DHH** around the next spoke. Continue left to right across the row in the same way (see Fig. 19a). When you get to the outer spoke, bring the other cord outward to the left and encase it along with the outer spoke when making the final **DHH** of the row (see Fig. 19b).

Fig. 21

5. Position the pin with the big bead to the top. Bring the remaining **KC** (Knotting Cord) behind the spoke and downward to start the next row (see Fig. 20). Make a **DHH** around the spoke (and any leftover weavers).

6. Working from right to left across the row, make **DHH**s around each of the spokes (see Fig. 21).

Color Band #4

Fig. 22

1. Attach a 20" length of 28 or 30g. wire to the outer left spoke by wrapping it around once (encasing the leftover weavers).

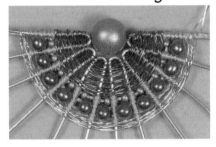

2. Make 3 rows of twined wire. Wrap one of the wire ends once around the outer spoke, encasing the other wire, spoke, and leftover cord (see Fig. 22).

Color Band #5

Fig. 23

1. Fold a piece of 40" cord so that one half is 8" longer than the other. Attach it to the left outer spoke with a **MTK** positioning the longer cord on the outside (see Fig. 23). Apply "Fray Check" or clear nail polish to about 2" of the end of the longer cord. Go onto the next step.

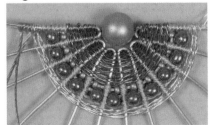

2. Make an **AHHch** (Alternating Half Hitch Chain) of 3 or 4 **HH**s. Attach the two cords of the chain to the next spoke, making sure to keep the longer cord to the outside (see Fig. 24).

Fig. 24

3. Continue across the row in the same way. When you get to the opposite end of the row, make a **DHH** around the outer spoke (and any leftover weavers of cord & wire) with the shorter cord (see Fig. 24).

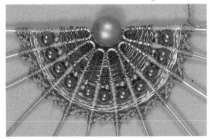

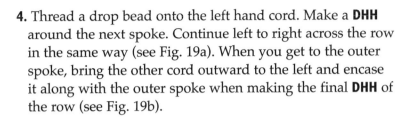

Project Eight

Fig. 25

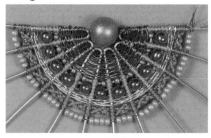

Fig. 26

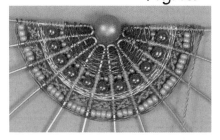

Fig. 27

Fig. 28

4. Bring the shorter cord parallel with the spoke, aligning it with the spoke and leftover cords/wires. Make a tight **DHH** around them with the longer cord.

5. Cut off all leftover weavers flush with the outer edge of the **DHH** (leaving the longer tail of cord uncut). Cut off any leftover weaver cords/wires next to the outer edge of the **MTK** at the beginning of the row (if there are any).

Color Band #6

1. Take a 26" length of 28 or 30g. wire and attach it at it's center to the left outer spoke by wrapping it around the spoke once. Bring the two equal lengths of wire together and twist them twice (see Fig. 25).

2. Thread 3 or 4 seed beads onto the wires and push them up over the twisted area. Bring one of the wires over and one under the next spoke. Twist the wires again and add seed beads. Continue across the row in the same way (see Fig. 25).

3. Bring the remaining weaver cord from Color Band 5 parallel to the right outer spoke and encase it along with the spoke when turning the piece to begin twining the next row. Do not cut it off!

4. Make 2 rows of twining with the same wire weavers. Secure each of the wires at the outer spoke by wrapping them completely around the spoke (and cord) one time.

Color Band #7

1. Position the piece with the spokes facing downward. Bring the cord down behind the outer spoke (see Fig. 26).

2. Make a **DHH** encasing the spoke and the 2 wire weavers. Cut off one of the wires flush with the outside of the **DHH** (be careful not to cut into the cord!).

3. Make another **HH** encasing the spoke and the one remaining wire. Carefully cut off the wire flush with the outside of the **HH** (see Fig. 26).

     Wired Micro-Macramé Jewelry

4. Thread a 4 mm bead onto the cord followed by a seed bead (see Fig. 27). Make a **DHH** around the next spoke. Thread on another 4 mm bead followed by a seed bead, make a **DHH** around the next spoke. Continue the row in the same way until you come to the fifth spoke from the right.

5. Make a **DHH** around the fifth spoke. Thread a seed bead, a 4 mm bead, and a seed bead onto the cord. Make a **DHH** around the sixth spoke (see Fig. 27).

6. Thread a seed bead followed by a 4 mm bead onto the cord. Make a **DHH** around the next spoke. Complete the row in the same way (see Fig. 27).

7. After making a **DHH** around the outer left spoke, make an additional **HH** (making it a Triple **HH**). Bring the cord under the spoke in the opposite direction and thread it back through the first 4 mm bead and pull it tight.

8. Apply a dab of clear nail polish to back of the final **HH**s. Carefully cut off the remaining cord flush with the top of the bead.

Part 4 - Shaping the Spirals and Finishing

Note - The length of the spirals is up to you, but here's what I suggest:

1. Position the piece with the spokes pointing upward. Curl the right-facing spirals at the tips of the spokes inward, leaving about $\frac{1}{4}$" of straight wire (see Fig. 28).

2. Curl the left-facing spirals at the tips of the spokes inward, leaving about $\frac{3}{8}$" of straight wire.

3. Cut each of the outer spokes to 2". Curl them in tight downward facing spirals (see Fig. 28).

Attaching a Pin-Back

4. Cut a 10" length of the same wire as was used in Color Band 4. Wrap one end of it several times around shank of the pin-back on the hinge end.

5. Flip the piece to the back and position the pin shank in the center, over the 4th Color Band.

6. Thread the wire onto a narrow sewing needle, and attach (sew) the pin-back to the piece with the wire, hiding the wire at the front within the wires of Color Band 4. Tuck the wire ends under the pin-back and cut off any excess.

Dynasty Pendant

The nesting wires in this pretty pendant reminded me of motifs I've seen in Asian art forms. It looks equally good when it's hung with the wires arranged vertically or horizontally. It could also easily be converted to a pin, with a pin back sewn to the back.

Materials

Wire:
- (25") 18 gauge round wire

Cord:
- 18g. Nylon Cord - 10 lengths @ 24"

Beads:
These beads were used in the example. Others may be substituted.
- (36+) 11° Japanese seed beads
- (1) 16" strand of 6 mm crystal rondelles
- Metal spacers
- 4 mm druks

Other:
- Hook and Eye clasp (or 4.25" of 16g. wire to make one)
- #10 sharps beading needle
- Nymo D or similar thread that matches the color of the cord

Optional - 1.25" X 1" piece of ultrasuede for lining the back
- 8 or 10 lb. Fireline

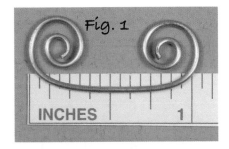

Fig. 1

Fig. 2

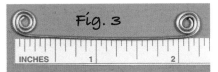

Fig. 3

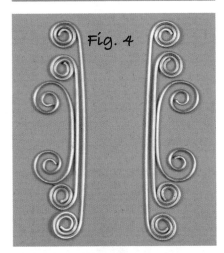

Fig. 4

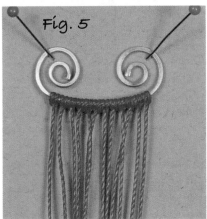

Fig. 5

Part 1 - Shaping the wires

1. Cut (2) 3.5", (2) 4", and (2) 5" lengths of wire. Shape the ends of the 3.5" wires into loose spirals, gradually curling one end and then the other until the spirals are equal and the finished length is approximately 1" (see Fig. 1).

2. Shape the 4" wires into tighter spirals, starting the loop of the spiral approx. $\frac{1}{3}$ way down from the tips of the round-nose pliers. The finished length should be approximately $1\frac{5}{8}$" and fit around the 3.5" wire form (see Fig. 2).

3. Shape the 5" wires into the same type of spirals as above. The finished length should be approximately 2.25" and should fit around the 4" wire form (see Fig. 3).

4. Lay out the wires on the table with one group on the left and one on the right. Check to see that they all are the correct lengths and forms (see Fig. 4). Optional - Flatten the wire forms with a chasing hammer if desired.

Part 2 - Directions for Knotting

1. Row 1 - Set aside one group of wires for now. Attach 6 cords to the 3.5" form (spirals facing up) with **MTK**s (Mounting Knots) (see Fig. 5).

2. Row 2 - Position the 4" form just below the 3.5" form and center it. Attach it to the other piece with **DHH**s (Double Half Hitches). **Tip** - I find it easiest to start at the center of the row. Make a **DHH** with the left/center cord, then a **DHH** with the right/center cord. Then switch back to the next cord on the left, then over to the right, etc... always working out towards the sides. This will help to keep the row close and tight to the previous row. If the wire becomes off-center, slide it back into position (see Fig. 6).

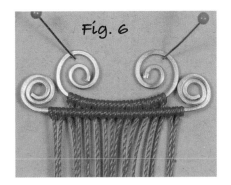

Fig. 6

Project Nine

3. Add another cord at each end of this row with **MTK**s. This will increase the warp (vertical hanging) cords to 16.

4. Row 3 - Position the 5" form just below the 4" form (spirals facing up) and center it. Attach it to the other piece with **DHH**s (see Fig. 7).

Note - I will refer to the warp cords as #1 - 16 according to their sequence from left to right.

5. Row 4 - Make a total of 4 **SQK**s (Square Knot) across the row grouping together Cds #1 - 4, #5 - 8, #9 - 12, and #13 - 16 (see Fig. 8).

6. Thread (1) 11° seed bead onto each of Cds #3 - 14 and push them all the way up next to the **SQK**s.

7. Row 5 - Make **SQK**s with Cds #3 - 6, #7 - 10, and #11 - 14 (see Fig. 9).

8. Thread (1) 11° seed bead onto each of Cds #3 - 14 and push them all the way up next to the **SQK**s.

9. Row 6 - Make a total of 4 **SQK**s across the row using Cds #1 - 4, #5 - 8, #9 - 12, and #13 - 16 (see Fig. 10).

10. Row 7 - Repeat Steps #6 - 8 (see Fig. 11).

11. Rows 8 & 9 - Repeat Steps #5 - 8 (see Fig. 11).

12. Row 10 - Repeat Step #5 (see Fig. 11).

13. Row 11 - Attach the 5" wire form to the piece (spirals facing down) with **DHH**s (see Fig. 12).

14. Row 12 - Attach the 4" wire form to the piece (spirals facing down) with **DHH**s.

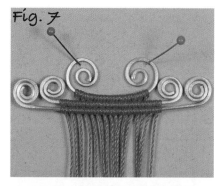

Fig. 7

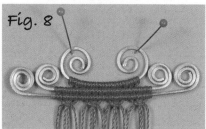

Fig. 8

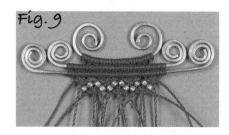

Fig. 9

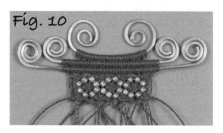

Fig. 10

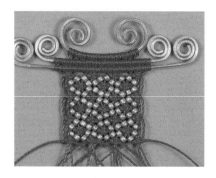

Fig. 11

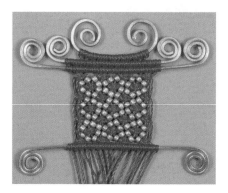

Fig. 12

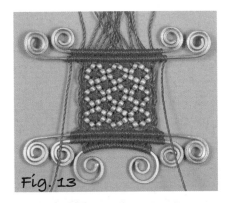

Fig. 13

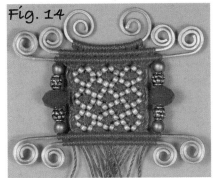

Fig. 14

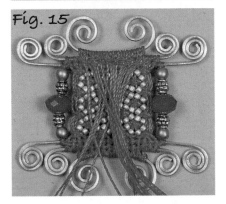

Fig. 15

15. Flip the piece so that the warp cords are facing upwards (see Fig. 13). Bring Cds #1 & 16 down behind the two wire forms and attach each of them to the 5" form with **DHH**s so that these 2 cords are hanging in the opposite direction of the other warp cords, at the outer edges.

16. Thread beads onto the 2 cords in any desired configuration, making them the same length as the space between the 5" wire forms (see Fig. 14).

17. Attach the 2 cords to the opposite 5" wire form with **DHH**s (see Fig. 14). If the adjacent bead has a big enough hole, thread the cord back through the bead to secure and hide it. Apply some clear nail polish to the back of the **DHH**. Cut off any excess cord flush where it exits the bead.

Note - If it is impossible to thread the cord back through the bead, thread it onto an embroidery needle and make one (invisible) stitch in the "ditch" between the two wires and bring the thread out again at the back. Make a very tight **OVK** (Overhand Knot). Apply some clear nail polish and let dry. Cut off the excess cord.

18. Omitting one cord on each edge, attach the remaining 12 warp cords to the remaining wire form.

19. Bring the hanging warp cords to the back and make a hem (see Fig. 15 & 16). Sew it down securely with a #10 Sharps beading needle and matching thread.

20. Sew a bead (or short stack of beads) onto each side, in the center of the 3.5" wire forms (see Fig. 17).

21. Optional - Cut a piece of ultrasuede to fit the knotted portion and sew onto the back of the piece.

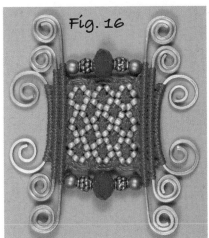

Fig. 16

Fig. 17

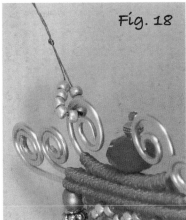

Fig. 18

Project Nine

Part 3 - Beaded Neck Chain

Note - In the following directions I use Fireline for the chains. You can make a chain with beading wire and crimps if you prefer that style.

1. Cut (2) 30" lengths of 8 - 10 lb. Fireline. Take one of the lengths and attach a beading needle.

2. Pass the Fireline through the opening in one of the two spirals at the top of the pendant. Thread on approximately (8 - 9) 11° seed beads and center them on the Fireline, so that they are positioned within the opening of the spiral (see Fig. 18).

3. Sew the Fireline once more through all of the beads (going in the same direction), creating a unified loop when tightened (see Fig. 19). The two halves of Fireline should exit at the same place at the top of the loop. Tie them together with an **OVK** next to the loop.

4. Thread the neck chain beads onto the two joined strands of Fireline, allowing 1" on each side for the length of the clasp. Take one of the threads off the needle, leaving just one.

5. Thread on (8 - 9) seed beads and one clasp part (see the "Petroglyph Pendant", Fig. 29, for clasp directions). Sew the Fireline once more through all of the beads (going in the same direction), creating a unified loop when tightened. Remove the needle and thread it onto the other strand of Fireline.

6. Going in the opposite direction of the first thread, sew around the loop of beads one time, exiting at the bottom of the loop (see Fig. 20).

7. Tighten the loop by pulling on both strands of Fireline until the loop is tight against the top neck chain bead. Make a very tight **SQK** with the 2 Fireline end threads around the neck chain threads (see Fig. 20).

8. Sew the threads down through 4" or more of the neck chain beads (see Fig. 20) and cut off the excess. Complete the other half of the neck chain in the same way.

9. Figure 21 shows the pendant with the wires arranged horizontally. Alternatively, the pendant can be hung with the wires arranged vertically as in Figure 16.

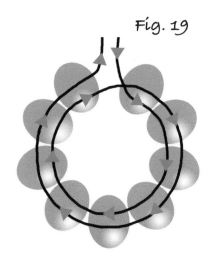
Fig. 19

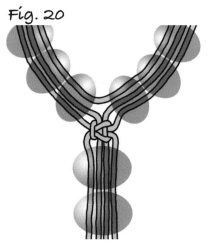
Fig. 20

Fig. 21

Petroglyph Pendant

Spirals can be found every-where in ancient rock art, from the petroglyphs of American Southwest to Celtic ruins. Apart from their symbolism, their pleasing shape is always easy on the eye. This colorful pendant features a promi-nent wire spiral centerpiece on a knotted half-circle design.

Materials

Wire:
- (2.5") 14 gauge round wire
- (18.5") 16 gauge round wire

18g Nylon Cord:
- 3 lengths @ 53"
- 2 lengths @ 46"

Beads:
The following beads were used in the exam-ple, others may be substituted if desired.

Knotted Section -
- (10) 4 mm drops
- (10) 3 mm rounds
- (20) 11° (Japanese) Color A
- (13) 11° (Japanese) Color B
- (40+) 1.5mm cube
- (13) 8°

Paddles and Neck Chain - assorted 4 mm - 8 mm

Other:
- (2) 5-6 mm jump rings
- 64" 8 - 10 lb. Fireline
- #10 sharps beading needle

Project Ten

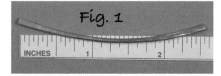

Fig. 1

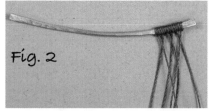

Fig. 2

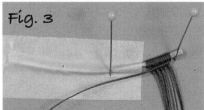

Fig. 3

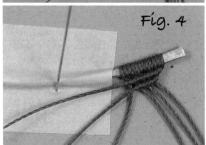

Fig. 4

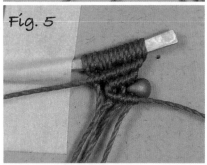

Fig. 5

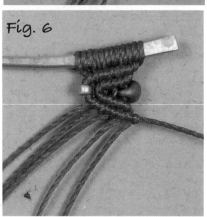

Fig. 6

Part I - Half-Circle Design

Outside Knotted Chain -

1. Cut a 2.5" length of 14g. round wire. Shape it into a very slight curve. Hammer slightly and splay the ends so that they are wider than the other part of the wire (see Fig. 1).

2. Double each of the 56" cords and attach them to the right end of the wire with **MTK**s (Mounting Knots) (see Fig. 2).

Note - I will refer to the cords as #1 - 6 according to their sequence from left to right. Cords may change sequence and therefore number from row to row.

3. Row 1 - Tape the wire to the board to hold it in place. Bring Cd #6 horizontally to the left and use it as the **AC** (Anchor Cord). Working from right to left, make **DHH**s (Double Half Hitches) around it with Cds #5 - 1 (see Fig. 3).

4. Row 2 - Bring Cd #6 (farthest on the right) horizontally to the left and use it as the **AC** for Rows 2 and 3. Working from right to left, make **DHH**s around it with Cds #5, 4, and 3 (see Fig. 4).

5. Row 3 - Thread a drop bead onto the far right cord. Bring the **AC** back around to the right and make **DHH**s with the same 3 cords as the previous row. This row should be at a slight angle to accommodate the drop bead (see Fig. 5).

6. Row 4 - Thread an 11° bead onto Cd #1 (the **AC** from Row 1). Bring it around to the right and following the angle of Row 3, make a row of **DHH**s with Cd #2 - 6 (see Fig. 6).

7. Thread a 3 mm (or you can use an 8° bead here) on Cd #2 and a 11° on Cd #4 (see Fig. 7).

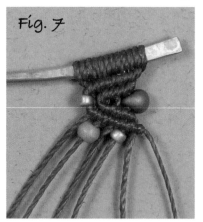

Fig. 7

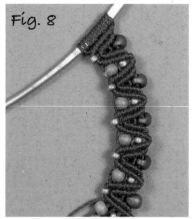

Fig. 8

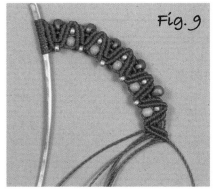

Fig. 9

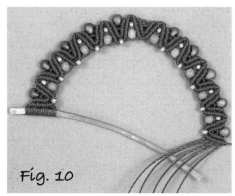

Fig. 10

8. Repeat Steps 3 - 7 four more times. Rotate and repin the piece as necessary to have the best angle for knotting (see Fig. 8).

9. Repeat Steps 3 - 6 one time omitting the beads (see Fig. 9). Repeat Step 7.

10. Complete the chain by repeating Steps 3 - 7 five more times (omitting Step 7 on the final segment) (see Fig. 10). There should be 10 drop beads on the edge.

11. Attach the six cords to the wire in the following way:

A. Attach Cd. #6 (the **AC** of the previous row) to the wire with a **DHH** (see Fig. 11). Bring Cd #6 to the left and parallel with the wire.

B. Treating Cd #6 and the wire like a single unit, make a **DHH** around them with Cd. #5. Bring Cd. #6 to the back of the piece behind the remaining warp cords and out of the way.

C. Treating Cd #5 and the wire like a single unit, make a **DHH** around them with Cd. #4. Bring Cd. #5 to the back of the piece and out of the way.

D. Continue working towards the left and attach all of the remaining cords in the same manner, encasing the previous cord and wire together as one unit and bringing the cord to the back of the piece before moving to the next cord. Cd. #1 will be the only cord that won't be encased along with the wire (see Figures 12 & 13).

12. Cut off all of the cords except Cds #1 & 2. Bring those two cords to the back and sew them down securely.

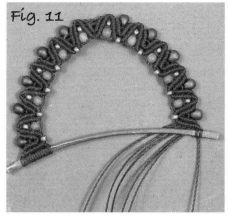

Fig. 11

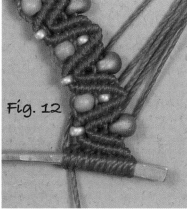

Fig. 12

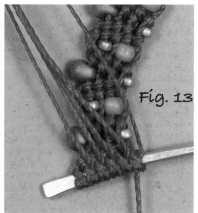

Fig. 13

Project Ten

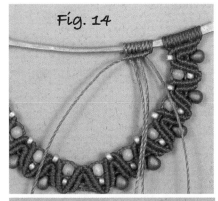

Fig. 14

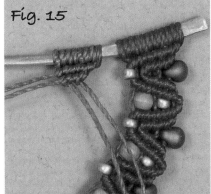

Fig. 15

Fig. 16

Inside Knotted Chain -

1. Double the two 46" cords and attach them to the wire with **MTKs**, positioning them to the left of the outside chain, leaving a small gap between the chains.

Note - I will refer to the cords as #1 - 4 according to their sequence from left to right. Cords may change sequence and therefore number from row to row.

2. Row 1 - Bring Cd # 4 to the left and using it as the **AC**, make **DHH**s around it with Cds #3 - 1 (see Fig. 14).

3. Row 2 - Bring Cd #4 (right outer cord) to the left and using it as the **AC** for Rows 2 & 3, make **DHH**s around it with Cds #3 & 2 (see Fig. 15).

4. Row 4 - Thread an 8° bead onto the right outer cord. Bring the **AC** from Row 2 back around to the right and attach the two cords to the **AC** with **DHH**s (see Fig. 16).

5. Thread an 11° bead onto the **AC** from Row 1. Bring the **AC** back around to the right and make a row of **DHH**s with the 3 warp cords. Thread an 11° bead onto Cd #2 (see Fig. 17).

6. Repeat Steps 2 - 5 six more times, omitting the final 11° bead in the last segment (see Fig. 18).

7. Position the piece with the wire at the bottom. Bring the cords behind the wire. Starting with the **AC** and working towards the left, attach the four cords to the wire with **DHH**s.

8. Reposition the piece with the wire at the top. Bring the leftmost warp cord to the left and down behind the wire. Make a **DHH** around the wire so that the cord now hangs downward (see Fig. 19).

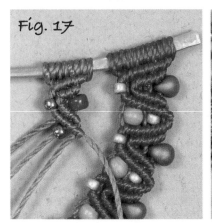

Fig. 17

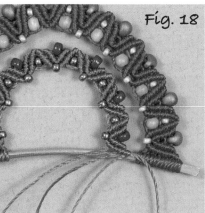

Fig. 18

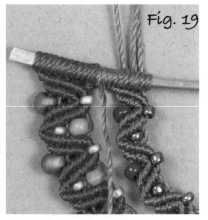

Fig. 19

9. Bring the next two warp cords to the back of the piece behind the chain and sew them down securely. Leave the rightmost cord as is, it will be used later (see Fig. 20). Cut off the excess from the 2 middle (sewn down) cords.

10. Thread 1.5 mm cube beads onto the cord that hangs in between the inner and outer chains, fitting the strand between the chains (see Fig. 20).

Fig. 20

11. Reposition the piece with the wire to the bottom. Attach the strand cord to the wire with a **DHH** in the space in between the chains (see Fig. 21). Bring the same cord to the right under the inner chain. Make a **DHH** with it around the wire to the right of the chain (see Fig. 22).

12. With the remaining cord from the other side of the piece make another **DHH** around the wire just to the left (moving the cord slightly closer to the center) (see Fig. 22).

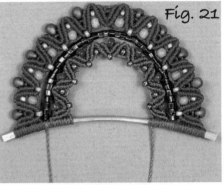

Fig. 21

Part 2 - Spiral Ornament and Eyepins

1. Cut a 12" length of 16 gauge round wire. Make a loose spiral, stopping when there is 2" of straight wire remaining (see Fig. 23a).

2. Grasp the remaining end within the largest part of round nose pliers. Make a short spiral in the opposite direction of the large spiral by wrapping the wire around the jaw of the pliers 1 and 1/3 times (see Fig. 23b).

3. Position the piece with the wire at the bottom. Lay the spiral on top. With each of the two cords, make a **DHH** at the top of the spiral on each side, wrapping the cord around the outer wire of the spiral and the lower wire joining them together (see Fig. 24).

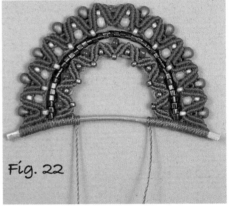

Fig. 22

Fig. 24

Fig. 23
A.

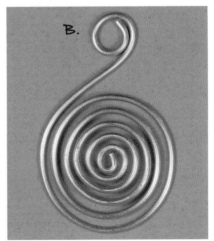

B.

Fig. 25

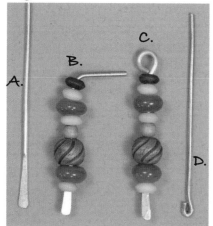

4. On each side - thread an embroidery needle onto the cord. Sew it from back to front to back (making one small stitch) just below the wire in the adjacent chain. Make an Overhand Knot at the back of the chain. Tighten well. Apply clear nail polish, let dry, and cut of excess cord.

5. Cut two 2" and one 2.5" lengths of 16g. wire. On each wire, hammer about ½" of one end flat, forming a "paddle" (see Fig. 25a). Or make a small loop instead of a paddle (see Fig. 25d).

6. Thread beads onto the 2" wires leaving ½" of wire at the top. Kink the wire(s) to the side above the top bead (see Fig. 25b). Curl the wire back to make a loop (see Fig. 25c).

7. Thread beads onto the 2.5" wire leaving ½" of wire at the top. Kink the wire to the front above the top bead. Make a loop that's perpendicular to the flat "paddle" (see Fig. 27).

Fig. 26

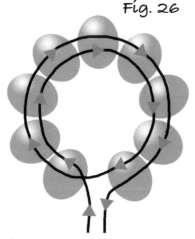

8. Anchor the wire of the spiral to the knotting at the center of the outer chain. Use a piece of spare cord and an embroidery needle and sew over the spiral's descending wire twice joining it to the knotting (see Fig. 29). Tie off at the back with a flat Square Knot. Apply clear nail polish, let dry and cut off excess cord.

9. Attach the center eyepin by passing it through the bottom spiral. Attach the 2" eyepins to each side of center with jumprings. Position the jump rings at the outer edge of the chain, 6 rows to either side of the center point (see Fig. 27).

Part 3 - Neck Chain

1. Cut one 32" length of 8 - 10 lb. Fireline for each side of the neck chain. On each, thread (9 - 11) 11° beads onto the thread and position them in the center. Pass the thread through the beads another time to form a circular loop (see Fig. 26).

2. Tie the 2 equal lengths of thread together as close as possible below the loop with an **OVK**. Thread any beads that you choose onto the 2 joined threads (see Fig. 29).

3. Sew the threads of the strands to the cords at the top/back of the knotted pendant at each side. Knot them off securely.

4. Attach the clasp to the top loops on each side (see Fig. 29).

Fig. 27

Hook and Eye Clasp (Fig. 28)

1. Hook -

A. Cut a 2.25" length of 16g. wire. Make a very small closed loop on one end. On the other end of the wire, make an attachment loop.

B. Bend the wire around a $\frac{5}{16}$" dowel or cylinder to make the hook.

C. Rotate the attachment loop with chainnose pliers so that it is perpendicular to the hook.

D. Flatten the hook section lightly with the hammer then go back and flatten the outer edge of the bend more distinctly.

2. Eye -

E. Cut a 2" length of 16g. wire. On one end make an attachment loop the same size as the hook's loop.

F. With large round nose pliers, curl the other end of the wire in the opposite direction, making a large loop that overlaps itself slightly.

G. Rotate the attachment loop with chainnose pliers so that it is perpendicular to the large loop.

H. Flatten the large loop lightly with the hammer then go back and flatten the outer edges more distinctly.

Fig. 28

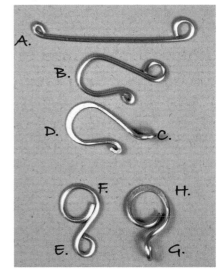

Fig. 29

Joan Reeder Babcock

is a fiber artist, jewelry designer, teacher, and author who has been creating one-of-a-kind jewelry and fiber art since 1988.

She is known for her unique style of blending cords, beads, and metal elements together, and specializes in the technique of "Cavandoli" or tapestry knotting. Her work has been featured in numerous fiber art and bead related books and magazines.

She is the author of "Micro-Macramé Jewelry: Tips and Techniques for Knotting with Beads" and a DVD, "Micro-Macramé & Cavandoli Knotting, Level One".

Joan lives in Santa Fe, New Mexico with her husband and business partner Jeff and companion cats Lily and Marley.

You can see her jewelry and fiber art at:

www.JoanBabcock.com
and
www.Micro-MacrameJewelry.com

Made in the USA
Lexington, KY
07 April 2014